# Doing Evangelism Jesus' Way

# Doing Evangelism Jesus' Way

## How Christians Demonstrate the Good News

Ronald J. Sider

Toll-Free Order Line: (800) 253-9315
Internet Website: www.evangelpublishing.com



Cover designed by Brad Sherman
Text edited by Dimples Kellogg

---

**Publisher's Cataloging-in-Publication Data**
***(Provided by Quality Books, Inc.)***

Sider, Ronald J.
Doing evangelism Jesus' way : how Christians demonstrate the good news / Ronald J. Sider.
p. cm.
LCCN 2003107663
ISBN 1-928915-49-3

1. Evangelistic work. 2. Christian life. 3. Church and social problems. I. Title.

BV3790.S549 2003 269'.2
QBI03-200624

---

Printed in the United States of America
03 04 05 06 07 / 5 4 3 2 1

# Contents

To Dorothy Sherk

My gifted high school teacher,

and long-time and continuing encourager

# Acknowledgments

Various chapters of this book are excerpted from sermons which the author has preached over the past two decades. He gratefully acknowledges the sponsoring organizations' invitation to share these ideas in each of those settings.

**Chapter 1: Christ's Plan to Save the World**
Part of a Lenten sermon series at Eden Mennonite Church in Moundridge, Kansas, April 8–10, 2001.

**Chapter 2: The Essence of Christian Faith**
Originally part of a sermon entitled, "A Missing Link," delivered at Eastern Baptist Theological Seminary, Wynnewood, Pennsylvania, on September 21, 1982.

**Chapter 3: Holiness in a Relativistic Age**
Originally a sermon entitled, "Preaching Holiness in a Promiscuous Age," delivered at Eastern Baptist Theological Seminary in the early 1990s.

**Chapter 4: Putting the Kingdom First**
Originally delivered as the commencement address at the high school graduation of our son Michael from Christopher Dock Mennonite High School on June 7, 1986.

**Chapter 5: Staying Married in a Crazy World**
Adapted from a sermon entitled, "Fifty Years Together," delivered for the fiftieth wedding anniversary of David and Fannie Lichti, the parents of the author's wife, on May 10, 1989.

**Chapter 6: In Word and Deed**
Delivered as part of a Lenten sermon series at Eden Mennonite Church in Moundridge, Kansas, April 8–10, 2001.

**Chapter 7: If Christ Is Not Risen**
Delivered as part of a Lenten sermon series at Eden Mennonite Church in Moundridge, Kansas, April 8–10, 2001.

# Preface

This book originated with a series of Lenten sermons that a group of churches invited me to deliver at Eden Mennonite Church in Moundridge, Kansas, on April 8–10, 2001. I was delighted to accept that invitation for two reasons.

For one thing, this association of Mennonite and Methodist churches made me feel right at home because I have strong credentials in both groups. I am a member of a Mennonite church and have ministerial credentials in the Mennonite church, but I am also a member of the Brethren in Christ Church, which has very strong Wesleyan roots. So I can claim to be both Anabaptist and Wesleyan. And I do, with gratitude.

The second reason was related to that because I think that the vision of the early Anabaptists and the early Wesleyans came close to capturing what the gospel of Jesus Christ was all about. Both had a strong emphasis on the church as community. Both had a vigorous concern for the poor. Both had a longing to have the Holy Spirit transform believers into persons who truly imitate Jesus Christ. They had a passionate desire to spread the gospel everywhere.

The early Anabaptists, after all, were the first Protestant missionaries. They put Jesus Christ at the very center of their living and thinking. And their deepest desire was to let this Jesus Christ, whom they worshiped and loved, be the core of their life, and to obey Him and the Scriptures.

That is my deepest passion—to be unconditionally submitted to Jesus Christ and to the Scriptures. You may not agree with everything in these pages. That's all right. But if you don't, I only ask that you help me to see how anything that I say is not faithful to Jesus Christ and the Scriptures. Then I'll be eager to change it as fast as I can!

Ronald J. Sider
Eastern Baptist Theological Seminary
Wynnewood, Pennsylvania

# 1. Christ's Plan to Save the World

Someone has imagined an astonishing conversation between Jesus and the archangel Gabriel when Jesus returned to heaven.

"Well, how did it go?" Gabriel asked Jesus. "Did You complete Your plan? Did You save the world?"

Jesus said, "Well, yes. . .and no.

"I modeled a godly life for about thirty years. I preached to a few thousand Jews in a little corner of the Roman Empire. I died for the sins of the world. I promised that those who believe in Me will live forever. Then I burst from the tomb to convince 120 frightened followers that My life and My story were God's way to save the world. And then I gave those 120 the Holy Spirit, and I left them to finish the task."

"You mean Your whole plan to save the world depends on that ragtag bunch of 120 ex-fishermen, prostitutes, and tax collectors?" Gabriel asked in astonishment.

"That's right," Jesus replied.

"But what if they fail?" Gabriel insisted. "What's Your backup plan?"

Slowly, Jesus said, "There is no backup plan."

That's still true, my friends. Christ has no backup plan; you and I are it. His plan to save the world and change it is not one He decided to carry out through angels. He decided that you and I would do it.

Gabriel must have watched dumbfounded as that first motley crew of Christians set to work. They had little money, no education, and no political clout, but they loved Jesus with all of their hearts. They defied raging oceans and roaring lions to spread the Good News and live it. And the message spread like wildfire. Within three short centuries, they had conquered the most powerful empire that had ever existed.

As the centuries rolled along, Gabriel must have watched and marveled as Christianity spread west to Europe and north into Russia, south into Africa, and farther west to the Americas. Finally, in the explosive missionary efforts of the last two centuries, he saw Christian faith sweep across Africa and grow very quickly in Asia. The 120 Christians in the Upper Room had become more than two billion people in every country on the planet. Yes, without any backup plan Jesus' strategy really was working.

But as Gabriel peered more carefully, an old anxiety surfaced. Time after time in previous centuries, vast numbers claimed to be Christians without living what Jesus taught. Gabriel must have wondered, *Are the people who claim the name of Christ really much different from those who do not? How could the worst massacre of Jews in human history occur in Europe, the continent that had been "most Christian" for the longest time?*

Gabriel must have pondered the United States, too. Eighty-six percent of the people tell pollster George Gallup that they are Christians, while about 45 percent go to church on Sunday morning. But does their Christianity make any difference day by day? The United States has the highest divorce rate of any nation in human history. Moral relativism has invaded the minds of its people, even of Christians. The United States jails the highest percentage of its people of any industrialized nation. Violence and drugs stalk our cities. There are many Christians in American politics, but do they talk about the poor the way the Bible does? Do they make policies to alleviate the suffering of the poor?

Was Jesus Christ's strategy for changing the world really working? The picture wasn't entirely clear to Gabriel. Vast numbers of Americans called themselves Christians, but they seemed to live just like their secular neighbors.

Here and there, Gabriel could see people who were different—dramatically different—living like the first 120 disciples. He looked down into Chicago and saw Wayne Gordon in one of the poorest, most violent sections of inner-city Chicago. Soon after his conversion as a teenager, Gordon said, "God, I'll do anything You want me to do with my life."

Wayne Gordon had gone into the inner city, defying roaches and rats, break-ins and violence, to tell inner-city kids with virtually no hope of a decent education, job, or marriage that the Creator of the universe loved them and wanted them to live eternally with Him. Because Wayne followed Jesus' example of caring for the whole person, he started a tutoring program, a medical clinic, and recreational services. After twenty-five years, God has blessed Wayne's faith, prayer, and hard work with a thriving interracial church of about a thousand people and a $13-million-a-year program, transforming a whole section of inner-city Chicago.

Gabriel can see other committed Christians. There are hundreds of thousands of them scattered around the globe. Jesus is the center of their lives and joy. Everywhere they are leading people to Christ. They are throwing their arms around even the most needy. They are walking arm in arm with these broken people as Christ restores them to wholeness. Their ministries renew broken families, empower the poor, and transform violent neighborhoods. They correct environmental pollution. They work for freedom, peace, life, and justice in society. Again and again their labor and goodness are slowly improving whole communities.

*Yes,* Gabriel must think, *Jesus' strategy really does work when the people who claim the name are unconditionally committed to Jesus Christ. Even a small percentage of today's two billion Christians who claim to be committed to Christ could easily change the world in dramatic ways. The ravages of divorce could recede; almost everyone could enjoy a decent job and adequate income. Violence, racism, war could recede if only a fraction of Jesus' followers really practiced what Jesus preached.*

As Gabriel peers ahead into the next one hundred years of Jesus' astonishing game plan, he may be asking himself, *Will there be enough genuine Christians?*

That's the question I pose to you: Will there be enough genuine Christians?

## Marks of Genuine Christians

In my book *Living Like Jesus*, I spell out eleven marks of genuine Christians. Here are a few of them:

*Genuine Christians embrace both God's searing holiness and God's astonishing love*. I know from personal experience that the way to joy and happiness is found in the biblical truth about both God's holiness and God's mercy.

My wife, Arbutus, and I have lived together for forty years in what Richard Foster rightly calls "a mixture of ecstasy and halitosis." Mostly, it has been wonderful joy. But there have been times of struggle.

The most painful time came in our late thirties just when it's supposed to—midlife crisis and all. No, we did not commit adultery, but we did hurt each other very deeply. I must confess that my anger at Arbutus raised so strongly that I wanted to hurt her. Except for one thing, I would have had an adulterous affair. That one thing was this: I knew it was sin. I knew that I served a holy God who hated adultery. I knew I could not break my marriage vow and still look freely into the loving eyes of my Lord.

God's righteous commands protected me when my strength was very weak. The biblical truth about God's holiness guarded my steps and kept me from inflicting awful pain on the woman I love more than *any* other person in the world. That's not to pretend that we didn't hurt each other. Both of us did. Our marriage went through a serious crisis; there were days I wondered if it would survive. But precisely in those days, I learned something more profound about the Cross.

As I pondered the wounds that Arbutus and I had inflicted on each other, I realized that we had only three choices: One was to pretend that our sins against each other didn't matter very much. We could tell ourselves it was "no big deal." That would have been an absurd lie. Our treatment of each other hurt terribly.

The second possibility was to shout, "That's it! I'll never forgive you." That would have ended our relationship forever.

There was only one other possibility. I had to say to Arbutus (and she had to say to me), "Your actions were wrong. They hurt me deeply. But I love you. I love you so much that I will take the evil you have done into my heart and I'll forgive you. I can't say that it was nothing. That would be a lie. But I don't want to live forever estranged from you. So, I'll take the wounds that you have inflicted because of your betrayal, and I'll purify them with my love and my forgiveness."

That's what God was doing at the Cross. Sin is so serious that the death penalty has to be paid. God takes the death penalty upon himself at the Cross. God himself goes to the Cross because He loves us in spite of our sinful failures.

God embraces our sin and absorbs into the divine heart the evil we have done. God accepts the punishment we deserve, all because God wants to walk with you and me again face-to-face in openness and reconciliation. That's the most amazing solution to the problem of evil that the world has ever seen. No other religion dares to say that the Creator of the universe died for our sins. The Cross is the only satisfactory solution for the brokenness, the violence, the agony of our hurting world. But the Cross makes sense only if you understand the God revealed in the Bible: God is righteous Sovereign just as much as loving Father; blazing holiness is just as central to God's nature as His overflowing mercy.

Jesus taught us more clearly than anybody before or since that the awesome Creator of the galaxies is a tender, loving Father. He delights in our calling Him, "Papa!" At the same time Jesus repeatedly warned that sinners depart eternally from this holy God.

Many modern Christians would like to accept half of God. They would like to renegotiate God's revelation; they would like to substitute a new covenant and a new God who offers forgiveness without holiness. I think the modern church really wants a cosmic Santa Claus who produces wealth and health and happiness to bolster our good feelings and self-esteem. We would prefer a divine Buddy who smiles kindly at sin and says, "Ah, shucks, pal, we all mess up, don't we?" The modern church would like to forget sin. We'd like to rewrite our own guidelines for happiness. The modern church really wants to disregard the need for repentance and sanctification. We would like to replace holiness with happiness. It's reasonable to desire and pray for happiness, good health, and so on; but that isn't the purpose of Christianity.

The biblical God stands beckoning to you and me to return and rediscover who He really is. God summons us to bow in awe before His searing holiness as we praise Him for His astounding love.

*Genuine Christians know who Jesus really is and surrender every fiber of their being to Him.* Too many people in our churches don't really know the full biblical Christ. Some worship Jesus as God and Savior, then forget that He was the liberator of the poor, the friend of prostitutes, and the peacemaker. Other Christians claim to follow Jesus as the world's greatest ethical teacher and the most wonderful peacemaker of all time, then forget that He was true God as well as true man, the only way to salvation. Most Christians, no matter what they say they believe about Jesus, simply don't practice what He preached. Christians tend to mimic the world today. Too many Christians are almost as self-centered, almost as sexually promiscuous, almost as racist and materialistic as their unbelieving friends. Too many Christians worship wealth, commit adultery, file for divorce, and destroy the environment just like their unbelieving neighbors.

Mahatma Gandhi was undoubtedly the greatest Hindu of the twentieth century. As a young man, he seriously considered becoming a Christian. He loved the Jesus of the Gospels. But when he compared how Christians lived with what Jesus did, he turned away in disgust.

Jesus was a radical fellow. He gently ministered to all sorts of untouchable people, including lepers and prostitutes. He commanded His followers to love even their enemies. He warned that those who do not feed the hungry and clothe the naked will depart eternally from a living God. He also claimed to be the only Son of God. He died for the sins of the world.

The early Christians taught that Jesus wanted them to live the same way that He did. They knew the risen Lord in their lives gave them the power to do it. That's why the early Christians so astounded their pagan neighbors.

Paul summed it up when he wrote, "All of us, with unveiled faces, seeing the glory of the Lord as though reflected in a mirror, are being transformed into the same image from one degree of glory to another" (2 Cor. 3:18). Daily, Paul said, we look into the face of Christ because the spiritual veil has been torn aside and we reflect His glory. Day by day, we are being transformed and made more and more like Jesus Christ. Genuine Christians live like Jesus.

*Genuine Christians keep their marriage vows.* This is a tough topic. My wife is a family therapist, and week by week, I hear about the agony of Christian marriages coming apart.

But let me tell you a story about Uncle Jesse. After five years of happy marriage, tragedy struck when Aunt Lydia developed a mental illness. Uncle Jesse had to take her to the hospital in Hamilton, Ontario. At first, he checked with the doctors every week, thinking that soon she'd be well enough to come home. But one day a doctor said, "Your wife's not going to get any better. I think you should go home and start over. Take care of your girls and forget about this woman!"

Uncle Jesse said, "Well, Doc, I can go home and take care of the girls. I'm doing that. But I can't forget Lydia; she's a part of me."

For almost thirty years Uncle Jesse drove the forty or so miles to Hamilton about every two weeks to visit the woman whom he had promised to love for better or for worse, till death would them part.

After many years, the surgeons did a lobotomy on her brain, and she was much better. She came home for a little while, but she still was not well. One day, she wandered down to the farmhouse where my mom and dad lived. My dad helped Uncle Jesse take her back to Hamilton.

Many years later the doctors finally got her medication right. After twenty-nine years of mental illness, she was home. Sloppy appearance and religious indifference were clear signs that Aunt Lydia was not the woman whom Uncle Jesse had married, but he was delighted to have her home. She was cooperative, and for three years he gently cared for the woman he still thought of as his youthful sweetheart.

One Thursday, she felt sick to her stomach and developed appendicitis. Her appendix ruptured. Because of the lobotomy, she didn't get the physical signals she would have gotten normally, and she died.

I cried as I listened to Uncle Jesse tell that story. I said, "Did you ever feel angry at the Lord?"

He said, "I did right at first. I thought, *This isn't fair. She's only twenty-nine years old.* But that doesn't get you anywhere."

Then he said, "All those years, never once did I feel that she was a burden. Oh, she *was* a burden. But I never felt it was anything that I should be relieved of. I loved her and I did all I could."

I asked, "Do you think it would be harder today to do what you did thirty years ago? Divorce was seldom heard of then. Today, men abandon their wives for lots of reasons."

"I can't understand the modern attitude," Uncle Jesse said. "I chose a wife I thought was 'it.' Now why would I want to get rid of her for somebody else?"

"It looks like you've been asked to walk a tough road," I said.

"Yes," he replied, "especially if I had seen those thirty years ahead of me. I took her to the hospital with the feeling that she would be returning in three months or so, but it just didn't work that way. We walk with the Lord one day at a time."

Uncle Jesse made a vow before God, in the presence of Christian witnesses, with the woman he loved to live together in lifelong covenant, for better or for worse. It got a lot worse—but he kept that promise by God's grace, one day at a time.

Today's world is so different from Uncle Jesse's world that it feels like another planet. Nearly half of American couples break their marriage vows in adultery or divorce. We're doing to our kids what no generation in human history has ever done. The sociological studies pour out year after year, telling us that the Creator knew what He was talking about. Children need their parents, both of them. I don't think our society can survive many generations of what we're doing in our homes.

Now I don't mean to be simplistic. I know the agony and the pain of a troubled marriage. But many married couples walk away from their commitments far too easily. In a recent movie, the father tried to tell his little son why Mom and Dad were separating. He said, "Mothers and fathers just walk through the same doors at different times."

His little son spoke for millions of hurting kids when he replied, "Then why don't they wait for each other?"

If Christians today in large numbers followed Jesus rather than the world in our sexual practices and in our marriages, the Christian family would stand out in stunning contrast and appealing beauty. The Christian family would be like a cozy, inviting living room, warmed by a crackling fireplace in a frigid city paralyzed by a roaring blizzard.

In the next two decades, Christian marriage could be one of the most powerful ways that we share the gospel. Today's hurting, broken families long for something better. We can offer them what they seek, but only if we live it. Will enough Christians follow Jesus rather than the world in our marriages? Will enough Christians model such fidelity, such joy and wholeness and mutual responsibility in our homes and marriages, that the world will see and believe? That can happen only family by family, person by person.

God helping me, I pledge to treasure my wife and my children above work and money and fame. They have been God's best gifts to me, after His Son. Genuine Christians keep their marriage vows.

*Genuine Christians share God's special concern for the poor.* I won't say much here because I have written so much about this. But hundreds and hundreds of Scripture verses convey God's concern for the poor, and genuine Christians share that concern.

*Genuine Christians love the whole person the way Jesus did.* Some Christians focus on spreading the gospel and then neglect peacemaking and caring for the poor, while other Christians focus on peacemaking and justice and then neglect evangelism. (I'll say more about this later on.)

*Genuine Christians confess that Jesus is Lord of politics and economics.* The biblical Jesus is Lord of the boardroom just as much as the bedroom. Jesus is Lord of the Congress just as much as the church. Jesus cares about how you vote as well as how you pray. Genuine Christianity is not some personal, privatized affair that applies only on Sunday morning and maybe in the home, but then is ignored in the rest of life. The New Testament dares to say that the Man of Nazareth, the crucified and risen Savior, is King of Kings and Lord of Lords now. Genuine Christians know this, so they submit every corner of their lives to Him, whether their sexual lives or their business practices, whether their marriages or their politics. Genuine Christians confess that Jesus is Lord of all.

*Genuine Christians strive to make the church a little picture of what heaven is going to be like.* In the last book of the Bible, John painted a glorious picture of heaven. All tears, hunger, violence, hatred, and prejudice have fled. Standing around the throne praising God are a vast multitude that no one could number from every nation, tribe, and language.

By contrast, take a quick journey around planet earth. Racial prejudice and ethnic hostilities simmer in subtle prejudice and explode in deadly violence. Classes compete, the poorest starve, and the rich seek fulfillment in ever greater material abundance. Ugly hatreds rooted in race, in wealth, in gender, in ethnic identity destroy the human family.

So we have two pictures: a reconciled humanity in heaven, and a warring chaos on earth. Now I ask you to ponder the congregations that you know best. Are they more like the first picture or more like the second?

Thank God for wonderful reconciled congregations that overcome all the brokenness and hostility that constantly erupts! But too many congregations divide, just like unredeemed society, along lines of race, class, and ethnic background in all kinds of perceived disagreements. Such churches have no credibility with the world. Such churches misunderstand the gospel. Such churches have no power to transform society.

African-American evangelist Tom Skinner was quite right when he said, "The church is supposed to be a little picture of what heaven is going to be like." Why? Because at the core of the gospel is *reconciliation*.

The worst racial prejudice in the ancient world existed between the Jew and the Gentile. Paul told us in his epistle to the Ephesians that this dividing wall has been broken down in Christ. Paul dared to challenge Christians to put to death their hostility. Are you willing to let the gospel put to death whatever hostility is in your life?

At the Cross, Jew and Gentile were accepted unconditionally because Jesus took their place. As a result, their sinful hostility was overcome. That's the gospel. You simply cannot accept Jesus' forgiveness and then cling to your hostility toward other people. To do that is to deny the very center of the gospel.

Cliques in a church who refuse to forgive and embrace other Christians in their own congregation are a slap in the face of our crucified Savior, who died for our oneness and prayed for our unity. They also demonstrate a willful, rebellious turning away from our only hope of salvation.

Think about the early church. When pagan neighbors looked at that early Christian community, they saw a multiracial, multi-class community where Jews embraced Gentiles, masters welcomed slaves, the rich respected the poor, and men treated women as equals. Astonishing! Amazing! Think of the impact if our churches would look like that today!

I dream of something like this happening in Philadelphia. Philadelphia is divided along race and class, and all kinds of hostilities exist between the churches. I dream that we Christians would say together that our oneness in Christ means that we must overcome our human hostility. We must find ways to express this oneness clearly and visibly, to ourselves and to the rest of society. I dream that we would work together. I dream that we would say that it's wrong for poor Christians in the inner city to be struggling to have enough food and housing and education, while middle-class white Christians in the suburbs have an abundance of these things. And we would change all of that. I dream that we would come together in multiracial celebrations in our big arenas to worship together and celebrate our oneness in Christ. Is that unlikely? Yes! But is that unbiblical? Certainly not!

What would the world say? Unbelievers would be stunned. After a little while, when they see we're serious, they would come to Christ in new numbers. Genuine Christians make our congregations little pictures of what heaven will be like.

*Genuine Christians are servants.* What is the first thing that comes to mind when the gay community in Grand Rapids, Michigan, thinks about Jerry Falwell's former vice president? Well, a *Christianity Today* headline tells the story: "Ed Dobson Loves Homosexuals."

Dobson has been the pastor of Calvary Church, the largest evangelical church in Grand Rapids, since 1986. He knows absolutely that homosexual practice is sin. But a woman who had grown up in that church once wrote to Ed Dobson and said, "My son is in Grand Rapids. I'm afraid he's dying. Would you visit him?"

The young man was dying of AIDS. So Ed Dobson visited him. And he thought, *What am I supposed to do?* He decided to visit the local AIDS center run by the gay community.

The director was absolutely astonished that the pastor of the largest evangelical church would show up there. But slowly, Calvary Church developed a variety of means to serve people with AIDS. A member of Ed Dobson's church is now on the board of the AIDS Resource Center. Calvary buys presents for families of people with AIDS, and the church buries people who have succumbed to AIDS if they have no resources.

It hasn't been an easy journey. Hate letters poured in the week after Dobson announced the church's new ministry to people with AIDS. One letter warned, "If you get involved with HIV AIDS, this church will be overrun with homosexuals."

The next Sunday morning, Dobson replied, "If the church gets overrun with homosexuals, that will be terrific! They can take their places in the pews right next to the liars, the gossips, and the materialists." At the end of that message, Dobson said, "When I die, if someone stands up and says, 'Ed Dobson loves homosexuals,' then I will have accomplished something constructive with my life."

An editorial in the gay newspaper of Grand Rapids explicitly acknowledged that Calvary Church believes that practicing homosexuality is a sin, but thanked Calvary for inviting gays and lesbians to the church's services. Nobody in the homosexual community misunderstands Calvary's stance, but everyone knows that Pastor Ed Dobson and that church are gentle servants to people dying with AIDS.

### *Jesus Is A Servant*

At the center of Christianity is a Servant. Jesus insisted that He came not to be served, but to serve. Too often, Christians have failed to combine servanthood with truth. Too often, we have been ferocious in attacking sin but not gentle in loving sinners. Too often, our evangelism has come mixed with Western cultural arrogance and oppressive colonialism rather than immersed in Christlike acts of service and care. Too often, our political engagement has been a self-serving demand for power rather than a servant's voice for the weak and the needy. Too often, we have failed to imitate our Servant King.

We fundamentally distort Jesus' gospel and Jesus' claims unless we see them coming from a humble Servant. Jesus did claim to have divine authority to forgive sin. He did claim to be the unique Son of God. He did claim to be the long-expected Messiah. He did dare to declare that no one comes to the Father but "by Me." But He said all of that as a humble Servant, tenderly ministering to lepers and prostitutes.

Jesus' gospel is what this broken world needs. Biblical ethical standards are what our crazy society longs for, even though it doesn't know it. But this society will never be able to hear us unless we speak our message as servants.

Imagine the impact if the first thing that radical secular feminists thought about when someone mentioned biblical pro-family men was that deeply committed Christian husbands keep their marriage vows, engage in mutual submission, and tenderly serve their wives as Christ served the church. Imagine the impact if the first thought that occurred in the gay community when the word *Christian* came up was that those biblical folk condemn gay bashing and stand for justice on behalf of all people, including gays. Imagine the impact if the dominant impression of Christian voices in our communications media was unswerving championship for the poor and the voiceless. Imagine the impact if the first thought that occurred to non-Christians when the topic of evangelists came up was that all the evangelists they knew, even those on TV, were walking with the broken, serving the poorest, and living modestly so they could share with the needy. Genuine Christians imitate the Servant they worship and adore.

What would happen if even a quarter of the people who claim to be Christians actually lived like Jesus? Only God knows! But dream along with me as I imagine what Gabriel might see in the next hundred years.

I believe this new century could leave even Gabriel dumbfounded with joy. I can picture Gabriel marveling with astonishment as more and more Christians surrender unconditionally to the risen Lord, as they open their total beings to the fullness of the Spirit. They live as Jesus did; they care about the whole person, as Jesus did. By the millions, broken prostitutes and self-centered middle-class Christian materialists are radically and beautifully transformed. On every continent, growing congregations of faithful believers flourish. In every country, city, and village, Jesus' devout followers eagerly invite people to accept the Lord whom they adore. Then they patiently walk with these new Christians, offering God's tough love that transforms mangled lives into whole persons.

Imagine a century in which for the first time, vast numbers of Asians embrace Christ. China slowly becomes more free and just. A huge minority of its 1.25 billion people become disciples of Jesus. Africa becomes the continent where not only the highest number of people are Christians, but they actually follow Jesus most faithfully. Revival sweeps across North and South America, renewing tired, lukewarm, dying churches. Faithful Christians provide the moral leadership that slowly blesses Russia with freedom and justice. Even Western Europe, where Gabriel watched in horror in the twentieth century as Christianity almost disappeared, now enjoys a resurgence of biblical faith.

I imagine that as Gabriel watches with joy and amazement, he realizes that no new magic formula has been employed. This marvelous growth is not due to some new management technique or some technological breakthrough. As Gabriel examines this global explosion of Christian faith, the secret becomes crystal clear: Somehow, in God's grace, tens of millions of contemporary Christians truly live like Jesus. They love Jesus with all of their hearts and minds and strength. They surrender every fiber of their beings to Him. They imitate His love for the whole person. No matter what the cost, they give themselves and their resources to empower the poor and bind up the battered. Constantly, eagerly, passionately, they share their very best treasure—Jesus the Savior—inviting others to embrace His forgiveness and His healing. Then they teach these new believers what they wholeheartedly seek for themselves, namely, to let this glorious God and Savior become the unconditional Lord of every corner of their lives.

The result is stunning. In spite of tragic imperfections, tens of thousands of congregations actually begin to look like what heaven will be. In spite of painful failure, tens of millions of Christian marriages overflow with contagious joy and integrity. And in spite of wrenching injustice, whole societies become more free and fair. Tens of millions every year discover the incredible joy of personal faith in Jesus Christ.

Gabriel is astonished at the resulting beauty and goodness. Even more, he marvels at the simplicity of God's plan.

All it takes to spread the gospel, renew the family, restore the church, and reform society is a small band of genuine Christians as dedicated to Jesus Christ as the first 120 were.

As Gabriel watches the impact of the twenty-first-century church, he's astonished to realize that genuine Christians are still just a minority of those who claim the name. But that minority has an awesome power. The reason is simple: Day by day, they look into the face of Jesus Christ and whisper quietly, Lord, there's nothing I want so much as to be *more like You. And if You will give me the power, I'll do anything You want me to do with my life.*

## 2. A Missing Link

American Christians are a lot like the rich young man in Matthew's gospel. If church attendance means anything, ours is one of the most devout nations on earth. But when we look at our budgets—both our personal budgets and our national budgets—we see that mammon is our real God. Without much concern or guilt we let thirty thousand children in the world die every day of starvation. Americans spend more money on chewing gum each year than American Christians spend on worldwide evangelism. Truly, it is very hard for a rich person to "seek first the kingdom of God" (Matt. 6:33).

And we persist with our religious rituals and cultic rigamarole in spite of the warning of Micah. If the prophets made anything clear, they taught us that worship in the context of neglect of the poor and oppressed is an abomination to Yahweh. Micah asked,

> What does the LORD require of you
> But to do justice, and to love kindness,
> And to walk humbly with your God?
> (Mic. 6:8)

God said through the prophet Amos,

> I hate, I despise your festivals,
> And take no delight in your solemn assemblies,
> Even though you offer me your burnt offerings,
> and grain offerings,
> I will not accept them. . . .
> Take away from me the noise of your songs;

I will not listen to the melody of your harps.
But let justice roll down like waters,
And righteousness like an everflowing stream.
(Amos 5:21–24)

God says to us: "I hate your prayer meetings and Sunday schools; I puke at your charismatic fellowships and sophisticated liturgies because you neglect justice. You haven't really created justice for African Americans, Mexican Americans, or women, not to mention the hundreds of millions of poor folk in developing nations." If Amos and Micah were truly God's prophets, then the worship of many of our churches is an abomination to God.

The answer, I believe, lies in a recovery of the radical New Testament understanding of the church. The church is Jesus' new messianic community, living now by the power of the Spirit, the radical new values of Jesus' kingdom. In that new Spirit-filled, redeemed society sisters and brothers care for each other. They are available to and accountable for each other. That accountability extends, Paul said, as far as gentle, but firm, spiritual rebuke and church discipline in the body of Christ. I know that seems like a terrifying idea to contemporary Christians seduced by modern individualism, who protest, "My personal life is none of your business, thank you." But Paul said that if we see a brother or sister falling into sin, we must first search our motives, then weep and pray to the Lord, and finally, go and talk directly with the person. That has direct application to all of us—when, for instance, we see a marriage beginning to disintegrate or when we see someone going way beyond Paul's suggestion to take a little wine for the stomach's sake. I believe that the church—if it would truly function as Jesus' new, revolutionary community of caring brothers and sisters—would be exactly what our materialistic, unjust world needs.

We sometimes become confused about the essence of Christian faith. Seeking justice for the oppressed is a central Christian responsibility, but it is not the essence of Christian faith. The same is true of correct theology and liturgical practice. Theology and liturgy are important, but they are not the essence of Christian faith.

The essence of Christian faith is a living, personal relationship with Jesus Christ. The essence of Christian faith is an I-Thou encounter with the Creator of the galaxies who became incarnate in the carpenter of Nazareth. Christian ethics is important, but many people who have a dreadfully inadequate understanding of Christian ethics and frequently sin in this area are still forgiven by God's grace and have a living relationship with Jesus Christ.

Correct theology is so important that people who deny basic biblical doctrines such as the deity and resurrection of Christ and God's special concern for the oppressed ought not to be in positions of leadership in the church. But right theology does not make one a Christian. Only a personal encounter with the risen Jesus does that. The essence of Christian faith is not social justice or correct theology or liturgical beauty; it is a personal encounter between the infinite, divine Person and each of us finite persons.

Some argue that Micah was saying just the opposite. They contend that Amos and Micah meant to say that God has no interest in religion. Justice for the oppressed is all that matters. In *Marx and the Bible*, to take one example, Jose Miranda argues that knowing Yahweh is nothing more than seeking justice for the oppressed. Miranda even goes so far as to argue that Jesus Himself had no interest in cultic activity like prayer. Saying that justice is the essence of Christian faith is a fundamental distortion of both the prophets and Jesus. Certainly, they made the radical claim that religious practice divorced from a concern for the poor and oppressed is an abomination to God. But they never reduced Christian faith to a mere concern for justice.

What do I mean when I say that the essence of Christian faith is a personal relationship with the risen Christ? I do not mean that Christian faith is merely an individualistic affair between the believer and God. Please don't confuse this emphasis on personal encounter with individualism. Genuine Christian faith includes a corporate experience of God in the body of Christ. But every person who is truly a Christian (rather than just a nominal believer) has entered into a living, personal relationship with God.

At the heart of Christian affirmation is the incredible claim that the source of all being in the universe is an infinite Person who wants to have a personal relationship with finite persons. Everywhere in the Scriptures we see this emphasis on personal encounter. The Scriptures use the most daring anthropomorphic language about God: God speaks, commands, promises, becomes angry, and forgives. God is Father; God is Mother. This personal God enters into covenant—a commitment between persons. Therefore, it is significant that both the Old and the New Testaments take the category of covenant as one of the central concepts to describe God's relationship with His people.

When God comes to give us His most complete disclosure of who He is, God himself becomes flesh. He comes as a person, not a book or a tree. And in that ultimate revelation when God comes to us in His Son, Jesus tells us that we dare use the most intimate of all personal language to think and talk about our relationship with God. We can address the Sovereign of the universe as *Abba*—"Papa" or "Daddy." The child's word of tender respect and close intimacy is the right word to use for God. In *The Other Side of Silence,* Morton Kelsey puts it this way: "Christians are told to turn to the very force that moves the sun and other stars and speak like small children, who need their father and call out 'Daddy.'"

We must balance this intimacy with a terrible sense of awe. The One we call Father, Daddy, is the One we worship as the all-powerful Creator of the galaxies and the sovereign Lord of history. We cannot manipulate Him. We are tiny, helpless specks of matter on a small planet in a small galaxy in the Milky Way. Incredibly, you and I can have a personal relationship with that awesome, almighty Being. That majestic, omnipotent Sovereign says, "Call Me Daddy." We can revel in the intimacy of a personal relationship with the living God without forgetting that the Creator of the galaxies comes and holds our hands.

I like the way G. K. Chesterton, in his book *Orthodoxy,* underlines the fact that the essence of Christian faith is personal encounter with the living God:

> Plato has told you a truth; but Plato is dead. Shakespeare has startled you with an image, but Shakespeare will not startle you with one anymore. But imagine what it would be like to live with such men still living, to know that Plato might break out with an original lecture tomorrow, or that at any moment Shakespeare might shatter everything with a single song. The person who lives in contact with the Living God is a person always expecting to meet Plato or Shakespeare tomorrow at breakfast (pp. 154–5).

I stress that the essence of Christian faith is personal encounter with the risen Lord because there is a danger inherent in gaining theological education or becoming overextended in work on the Lord's behalf. It is possible to get so caught up in excitement about Christian ethics, biblical studies, or systematic theology (although I must confess I have not seen too many people carried away with raptured excitement over systematics)—so caught up in the study *about* God—that you lose or weaken your actual relationship *with* God. Or you can get so absorbed in working *for* God that you neglect your relationship *with* God. Some individuals have told me that they have not grown in their personal relationship with God after they have assumed leadership positions in the church. Some have even confessed that they felt farther from God after a period of time in these positions.

Here are two suggestions for avoiding the danger. The first is to keep very clearly in mind the distinction between having knowledge *about* God or working *for* God and experiencing a personal encounter with Him. In *Christian Faith,* Hendrikus Berkhof has said that "the lowest reaches of hell are reserved for theologians who are more interested in their own thoughts about God than in God himself" (*Christian Faith,* p. 30). By all means, study Old and New Testament scholarship carefully; study Christian ethics; master systematic theology! But never forget that those disciplines are like road signs. Road signs point to the next town. They are not the town itself. Theology and ethics are indispensable road signs pointing toward the correct understanding and obedient practice of Christian faith. But they are not Christian faith itself. Christian faith itself is a living I-Thou encounter with God in Christ.

My second suggestion is that you make the inward journey of prayer and contemplation a central part of your life. This is not the only way to grow in a personal relationship with God, but it is an indispensable part of it. Prayer, I believe, is a crucial missing link in much modern Christianity. And nowhere, I fear, is it more absent than in modern Christian social action.

The only hope for our time is a new movement of biblical Christians who immerse their search for peace and justice in prayer and the presence of the Holy Spirit. Nuclear disarmament, the preservation of the family, the attainment of international economic justice, and the restoration of the sacredness of human life will involve fundamental changes in our society. There is no way any of that will happen, there is no way to avoid global disaster in the next few decades, unless God sends sweeping revival and Spirit-breathed action for peace and justice. Prayer has always been central to mighty movements of God. I am sure it still is.

There have been important social movements in recent decades, and many Christians have been involved in them. But there has not been a movement calling for fundamental social change that was immersed in intercessory prayer and a radical dependence on the Holy Spirit. It is a tragic fact that contemporary Christian social activists place less emphasis on prayer than do their counterparts doing evangelism. Richard Lovelace is right: "Most of those who are praying are not praying about social issues and most of those who are active in social issues are not praying very much" (*Dynamics of Spiritual Life*, p. 392).

## *Earlier Models*

That was not always the case. William Wilberforce and the other members of the Clapham Sect were the leaders in the British crusade to abolish the slave trade. Historians tell us that they immersed their political strategizing and lobbying in daily three-hour sessions of intercessory prayer. Later in the nineteenth century Lord Shaftesbury spearheaded a large number of social reforms, ending child labor and reforming the factories. When his son asked how he could do so many things at once, he replied, "By hearty prayer to Almighty God before I begin, by entering into it with faith and zeal, and by making my end to be His glory and the good of mankind." (Lovelace, *Dynamics*, pp. 381–2)

Charles Finney was the Billy Graham of the nineteenth century, and he was also a leading crusader against slavery. He insisted that long hours of intercessory prayer were central to his work. Finney would have appreciated what Helmut Thielicke has said of Martin Luther: He prayed four hours each day, "not despite his busy life, but because only so could he accomplish his gigantic labors." (D. Elton Trueblood, *The New Man for Our Time*, pp. 66–7)

If we are to learn how to pray, we must come to believe that Jesus meant what He said about prayer. Too many Christians do not believe Jesus' teaching about prayer. And when I read His words, I can hardly blame them! Jesus said some of the most astonishing, outrageous things about prayer. Listen to a few of them.

In Mark 11:23–24, we have these incredible words: "Truly I tell you, if you say to this mountain, 'Be taken up and thrown into the sea,' and if you do not doubt in your heart, but believe that what you say will come to pass, it will be done for you. So I tell you, whatever you ask for in prayer, believe that you have received it, and it will be yours."

When the disciples could not heal the lad with epilepsy, they asked Jesus for an explanation. Jesus pointed directly to their weak faith: "For truly I tell you, if you have faith the size of a mustard seed, you will say to this mountain, 'Move from here to there,' and it will move; and nothing will be impossible for you" (Matt. 17:20–21). The gospel of John contains these breathtaking promises:

> Very truly, I tell you, the one who believes in me will also do the works that I do and, in fact, will do greater works than these, because I am going to the Father. I will do whatever you ask in my name, so that the Father may be glori-

> fied in the Son. If in my name you ask me for anything, I will do it. (14:12–13)
>
> If you abide in me, and my words abide in you, ask for whatever you wish, and it will be done for you. (15:7)

We don't really believe Him. Surely, He must be exaggerating! For years I never took seriously these promises of Jesus. Slowly, however, I am beginning to think that perhaps He did mean what He said. My faith is still small, but it is growing. I am beginning to take seriously the fact that the One I confess to be God incarnate said again and again that whatever we ask in His name, He will give. If we truly believe that the carpenter from Nazareth was God in the flesh, then it is a very serious matter to doubt His oft-repeated promise that He will answer our prayers.

Jesus attached three important conditions to His promises. First of all, we must have faith. But that condition seems like another burden rather than a help. If I don't have faith, I cannot suddenly manufacture it.

How do we obtain the necessary faith? I still feel very much a first grader in the school of prayer. Yet in the past few years as I have struggled and cried to the Lord for the healing of broken marriages of close friends, I have seen Him answer some of those prayers in marvelous ways. As God did that, my faith has grown stronger. Furthermore, just remembering that my Lord tells me that He will answer my prayer has strengthened my faith.

***Prayer in Peacemaking***

I was meditating on Matthew 17:20–21 just after Hiroshima Day, pondering Jesus' promise that faith the size of a mustard seed would move mountains. Like a flash, the thought came: *Even, Lord, the prevention of nuclear war?* That seemed too much! The looming danger of nuclear holocaust is surely the most foreboding mountain looming over humanity today. But the answer came back clearly: Yes, even the mountain of nuclear weapons. Even that immovable mountain can be removed if My people pray." I believe Jesus means exactly what He says. And He is the Lord of the universe. Surely, then, we can believe that the terrible mountain of nuclear weapons will be removed if God's people would unite in persistent, believing prayer.

But a second condition is attached to Jesus' promise. We must be ready to obey. In John 15:7 Jesus made the sweeping promise to answer prayer only for those who walk in intimate, obedient fellowship with Him. We abide in Him as we commune daily with Him. We abide in Him as we keep His commandments, and one of His commandments is that we forgive others with the same reckless abandon that He forgives us. In fact, Jesus said that when we start to pray, we should first forgive others (Mark 11:25).

It is impossible to pray properly with resentment in our hearts toward other people. My wife and I had a quarrel one weekend. When I started to prepare a sermon the following Monday morning, I still felt anger and resentment toward Arbutus. I wanted to pray for God's guidance and help in the writing. It became quite clear, however, that I first had to let go of my anger at my wife before I could open myself in believing prayer for God's presence and direction. Obedience is inseparable from effectual prayer ( James 5:16; 1 John 3:22). If we want to pray for peace and justice, we also have to obey Jesus' command to be peacemakers and seekers of justice.

A third condition is that our sole aim should be to glorify God. Jesus said that whatever we ask in His name, He will do it. Why? So that the Father is glorified (John 14:12–13). That means that God will not answer self-seeking prayers. Our intention must be the glory of God.

If we start to believe Jesus' promises about prayer and begin to fulfill the conditions attached to them, the importance of prayer will become clearer and clearer to us. Prayer is the most significant way to work for peace and justice today. Prayer is not just something we do for our personal spiritual growth. Prayer is not merely a brief introductory invocation while the last persons straggle into the planning meeting for the nuclear freeze campaign. Prayer is the way we do our work. Prayer is the way we change the world. God in His sovereignty has decided that our prayers affect history.

In his book *With Christ in the School of Prayer*, Andrew Murray says that in prayer we are allowed to hold the hand that holds the destiny of the universe. By our prayers, we Christians are "to determine the history of this earth" (p.102–3). God wants to save the family. God wants more justice in society. God does not want to see His beautiful creation destroyed in a nuclear holocaust. And God wants to accomplish these things through your prayers and my prayers.

How incredible! Prayer is not incidental to peacemaking. Prayer is not peripheral to seeking justice for the oppressed. Prayer is a central part of how we do those things. Andrew Murray puts it well:

> As long as we look on prayer chiefly as the means of maintaining our own Christian life, we shall not know fully what it is meant to be. But when we learn to regard it as the highest part of the work entrusted to us, the root and strength of all other work, we shall see that there is nothing that we so need to study and practice as the art of praying aright.

### *Spiritual Warfare*

Another reason prayer is so central to the search for peace and justice is that the battle is also a spiritual one. We are not just dealing with arrogant politicians or nationalistic generals. We are also fighting against the demonic powers of Satan, who wants to destroy God's good creation (Eph. 6:12). Only by spiritual warfare, only by the power of the Holy Spirit sought through intercessory prayer, can we overcome militarism, injustice, and the disintegration of the family.

You may want to start by reading a couple of classics on prayer. Richard Foster's *Celebration of Discipline* is my first recommendation. Don't just read his book as an academic exercise; begin to apply his suggestions. Then follow Foster with Andrew Murray's *With Christ in the School of Prayer.*

Then you may want to set aside ten minutes and work up to thirty or forty-five minutes. You may discover that you're more effective at a certain time of the day; whether it's morning or evening doesn't matter—just that you try to have a regular time each day. Don't be legalistic about this, however. Missing a day is no big deal. But if you discover that you are finding time only once a week, then you know legalism is not your problem!

My prayer time is at the beginning of the day. For years I struggled with my busy schedule. Every morning the pile of "important, urgent" things was so great that I could hardly force myself to spare ten minutes to read and pray. Even when I did, my mind was preoccupied with the waiting responsibilities. Then the Lord allowed me to experience a very painful, difficult period in my life. The only way I survived was through crying out with agonized tears to the Lord. Those times of prayer, of telling God about my struggle, were times of deep comfort. As a result, I came to enjoy that daily conversation with my Lord in a way I never had before. During that time, and since then, it has not been nearly as hard to set aside significant time at the beginning of the day for prayer and Bible reading.

Of course, each day of activity should be full of prayer. We can learn how to live at two levels.

At one level we can be talking with friends or colleagues at work; at another level we can be breathing short prayers to God for ourselves and others. But it is still true—at least for me—that nothing takes the place of regular times set aside exclusively for conversation with our Divine Lover.

Breath prayers can be helpful. In his book *The Breath of Life*, Ron Del Bene suggests that each person select a short, one-sentence prayer to breathe to God many times each day. This prayer should focus on a central desire and concern in your life. During lulls at work or school, while driving or eating, you can breathe your short prayer to God. I wish Christians in the peace movement would adopt a breath prayer like the following: "Lord Jesus, please remove the mountain of nuclear weapons." Ask yourself what God would do if a few million Christian peacemakers breathed that prayer to Him a dozen times a day for the next twenty years.

A personal conversation with David Watson, a leading British evangelist, provides another practical suggestion for the biblical movement of peace and justice today. When I talked with him years ago, he said God had led him to pray daily for the gift of evangelism and God granted him that gift. He told me that he believed I should pray regularly for the gift of Spirit-filled work for peace and justice. I wish that every Christian concerned with peace and justice would do the same. Only God knows what a few million Spirit-filled biblical peacemakers and social activists would accomplish by God's grace.

In personal prayer, we should pray for specific things in the area of peace and justice. Each day let's ask the Sovereign of history to restrain the powers that want to destroy God's lovely creation by a nuclear holocaust. Let's pray for reconciliation between Christians, Jews, and Arabs in the Middle East. Let's pray for an end to starvation and a more just international economic order.

Group prayer is also necessary. More and more local groups of Christians scattered across the world are working for peace and justice. I dream of each group learning in a new way how to immerse its common activity in hours of intercessory prayer. In our committee meetings devoted to mapping out strategy, could we devote half as much time to seeking guidance from the King in prayer as we do in discussion with each other?

### *A New Praying Movement*

Imagine a group of Christians working on a nuclear freeze campaign in their city. The most sophisticated strategy and hard work would be combined with long sessions of group prayer as well as private prayer by all the individuals involved. At particularly important times when key decisions needed to be made, there would be all-night prayer chains. As some members visited the mayor and asked for his support, others would gather to pray. On the night before the election, prayer chains would intercede throughout the night for the transforming presence of the Holy Spirit.

The same sense of prayer and radical dependence on the Holy Spirit would pervade regional and national peace and justice conferences. Surely, we are not too secular to make our conferences on peace and justice a little more like the old camp meetings where Christians interceded all night (as Jesus did) for the radicalizing presence of the Holy Spirit?

Prayer, I hope, will become the trademark of a new movement for peace and justice. If that happens, American society could recover a commitment to the sacredness of human life and the sanctity of the family. If that happens, affluent Americans could join people in developing nations in a new partnership for global justice. If that happens, our children could even be spared nuclear holocaust.

But that will happen only if each of us resolves to draw nearer to God. That will happen only if each of us understands that the essence of Christian faith is a personal, living relationship with the risen Lord. That will happen only if each of us nurtures that relationship with God in Christ through regular prayer and costly obedience. As that happens, you and I, through our prayers, can change the course of world history. Let's seize the missing link of prayer, believing that it is as strong as Jesus said it is.

> Jesus said to him, ". . .All things can be done for the one who believes." Immediately the father of the child cried out, "I believe; help my unbelief!" (Mark 9: 23–24)

# 3. Holiness in a Relativistic Age

In March 1990, I had the privilege of participating in Korea in a convocation of the World Council of Churches (WCC) dealing with justice, peace, and the integrity of creation. To my surprise, I was asked to chair one of the drafting committees. The discussion of sin in the draft document focused on the horizontal dimension—on the way that sin is a dreadful violation of our neighbor. With all of that, I agreed. But I pointed out that sin is also rebellion against a holy, righteous God, a violation of the just commandment of the Divine Judge who hates sin. Some committee members dismissed such language as paternalistic oppression, insisting that we focus only on God as loving, forgiving, accepting, nurturing. Others, I'm sure, ignored my plea for other reasons. But language about sin as a violation of God's holiness never made it into the final document.

A few weeks later, I was sharing my concerns about the contemporary church with a small circle of younger evangelicals. I talked about my fear that the radical subjectivism and relativism of the larger society were creeping into the church, even into evangelical circles. The dominant value of current American culture is that "what feels good to me is right for me." And God have mercy on anyone who dares to be so legalistic and medieval as to suggest that the righteous commandments of the Holy Creator of the galaxies are divine commands to me, no matter how I feel.

I won't try to describe what happened at that point. You can use your imagination. I'm still limping. We had quite a debate. One person almost walked out. Another person said that he wanted to focus all his attention on God's love. He said he held just two convictions: that he should love God with all his heart and his neighbor as himself.

Of course, I agreed that this double conviction (it wasn't clear that he would dare use the word *commandment*) is the heart of the whole matter. Our whole Christian life should flow out of gratitude for the astonishing, unmerited love of God in Christ. Because of that love, we can love God in return and our neighbor as well. But didn't Jesus and Paul go on to tell us that loving neighbor means obeying God's command not to violate the neighbor through adultery, robbery, gossip, or neglect of justice? In this small evangelical circle, as at the WCC convocation, I sensed a powerful hesitation to face the blazing holiness and righteous demand of almighty God who is just as well as forgiving and merciful. I'm afraid the modern world is making it hard for us to hear this aspect of biblical truth.

### *How Our Thinking Changed*

How has this happened? I can't summarize the intellectual history of the Western world in the next few paragraphs, so I can't answer that question adequately here. But I do want to point to a few key developments.

The Enlightenment's demand for absolute human autonomy is at the heart of the problem. Rejecting revelation as the source of ethics, Kant and the Enlightenment grounded ethics in autonomous humanity. Persons rather than God became the center of the universe. Then a variety of philosophical determinisms reduced ethical ideas to a mere relativistic by-product of this or that influence. Marx insisted that all ethical ideas were merely an expression of our economic life. Freud preferred to reduce our values to psychological conditioning. One secularist after another declared that lofty moral values are merely the result of our economic system or toilet training. As Bertrand Russell, one of the great secular philosophers of the twentieth century, said so eloquently: "Those who have the best poison gas will have the ethics of the future." In other words, all morality is relative.

And if you want to know how relativism works, just ask the sociologists. They will tell you that if you grow up in a society where the influential persons are witch doctors, you will believe in witchcraft. On the other hand, if you grow up among allegedly scientific secular humanists, you will think like secular humanists. All is relative.

Current American culture adds its own delightful spin to this prevailing relativism. Pop psychology assures us that whatever feels good is right for me. I have a right to self-fulfillment and if my spouse is not meeting my "needs," then I had better find someone else who will, or I may do terrible things to my psyche.

Christians quickly step forward to provide theological rationales for this prevailing relativism. One preacher largely ignores sin and develops a gospel of self-esteem. Another ignores justice for the poor and preaches a gospel of wealth. Some radical feminists dismiss language about God's justice and holiness as oppressive paternalism, while televangelist Tammy Bakker shares her spiritual wisdom in a book with the revealing title, *I Gotta Be Me*.

Mixed in with all this tragic nonsense is a set of confusions that further complicate the issues. Pluralism is confused with relativism, tolerance with subjectivism, and the universality of sin with the acceptance of sin.

I accept religious pluralism and vigorously defend everybody's right to believe what he or she chooses. I want to be tolerant of different views, in the sense that I respect those who believe very differently from the way I believe. But this does not mean that I believe one idea is as good as another. I can respect your right to think whatever you choose and still believe passionately that your ideas are dead wrong. Society should tolerate all ideas, but that does not mean that all ideas are equally true. But again and again, people confuse tolerance and relativism. A.W. Tozer has a powerful line that sums it up: "Truth is slain to provide a feast to celebrate the marriage of heaven and hell" (*Milk and Honey*, p. 2).

People also regularly confuse the universality of sin and the acceptance of sin. How many times have you heard somebody object to a clear biblical condemnation of some specific sin, whether economic injustice or sexual misconduct, with the plea: "But we are all sinners"? If I hear that confused response one more time, I may go theologically berserk. The fact that we all sin and fail to keep God's law does not mean that we should condone sin. It simply means that as we condemn sins such as racism or premarital sex, we also cast ourselves on God's grace to ask forgiveness for our own failures.

## *Conforming to Our Culture*

Probably the greatest temptation of the church over the ages has been slowly (and often unconsciously) to conform to surrounding culture rather than submit to the fullness of God's revealed Word. One aspect of biblical truth is affirmed while another is obscured and neglected.

God is certainly love—overwhelming, astounding love. That is at the core of the biblical revelation of the nature of God. But the Bible also tells us that God is holy and just. The Bible says God hates sin. Tragically, a variety of modern confusions make it difficult for contemporary Christians to hear this other side of biblical truth.

Every stream of biblical revelation affirms the holiness of God. As I quote a series of texts, let the awesome holiness of our almighty Creator sink deeper into your being. Listen to the prophet Isaiah describe his encounter with the Holy One:

In the year that King Uzziah died, I saw the Lord sitting on a throne, high and lofty; and the hem of his robe filled the temple. Seraphs were in attendance above him; each had six wings: with two they covered their faces, and with two they covered their feet, and with two they flew. And one called to another and said:

> "Holy, holy, holy is the Lord of hosts;
> the whole earth is full of his glory."

The pivots on the thresholds shook at the voices of those who called, and the house filled with smoke. And I said: "Woe is me! I am lost, for I am a man of unclean lips, and I live among a people of unclean lips; yet my eyes have seen the King, the Lord of hosts!" (Isa. 6:1–5)

After David raped Bathsheba and then murdered her husband, he repented and called on God for forgiveness. He could very rightly have stressed how terrible had been his violation of his neighbor, but Psalm 51 emphasizes his rebellion against a holy God. He said,

> For I know my transgressions,
> and my sin is ever before me.
> Against you, you alone, have I sinned,
> and done what is evil in your sight,
> so that you are justified in your sentence
> and blameless when you pass judgment.
> (vv. 3–4)

I have recently rediscovered the power and beauty of Psalm 119's praise and love for God's holy commandments. Here are just a few verses from the psalm:

> How can young people keep their way pure?
> By guarding it according to your word.
> With my whole heart I seek you;
> do not let me stray from your
> commandments.
> I treasure your word in my heart,

so that I may not sin against you.
Blessed are you, O Lord;
teach me your statutes.
With my lips I declare
all the ordinances of your mouth.
I delight in the way of your decrees
as much as in all riches.
I will meditate on your precepts,
and fix my eyes on your ways.
I will delight in your statutes;
I will not forget your word. (vv. 9–16)

Nor does the emphasis on God's holiness and demand for obedience end with the Old Testament. Those who do not obey Jesus' command to feed the hungry will hear the awful words: "You that are accursed, depart from me into the eternal fire prepared for the devil and his angels" (Matt. 25:41).

### *Holiness in the New Testament*

When Jesus prepared to leave His disciples and gave them the Great Commission, He told them that making disciples of all nations meant not just baptizing people but also "teaching them to obey everything that I have commanded you" (Matt. 28:20).

Paul, that great apostle of grace and freedom, never hesitated to underline God's holy hatred of sin. He wrote in Romans 1:18: "For the wrath of God is revealed from heaven against all ungodliness and wickedness of those who by their wickedness suppress the truth." He added in Galatians 5:19–21:

> Now the works of the flesh are obvious: fornication, impurity, licentiousness, idolatry, sorcery, enmities, strife, jealousy, anger, quarrels, dissensions, factions, envy, drunkenness, carousing, and things like these. I am warning you, as I warned you before: those who do such things will not inherit the kingdom of God.

God's Word is clear. God is loving and just, merciful and holy, nurturing and demanding, gentle with sinners and furious with sin. A promiscuous, relativistic age wants to hear only half of that. My question for all of us is this: Will we dare to declare and live God's holiness? People do not want to hear about God's tough love, but if we fail to speak about the full biblical word, we will ruin the church and deny our Lord.

Do you have the guts to say all that God's Word says about holiness, purity, and obedience to God's righteous commands? Of course, you don't. Neither do I. But we can decide as followers of the Word to do exactly that, then turn to God for the courage to say it—and to live it.

Only if we reach that point of unconditional personal consecration can we be examples of holiness. We cannot exhort other people to holiness while we live in impurity.

So my final plea is that you and I fall down together before our holy God and beg for both forgiveness and personal holiness: *Create in me a clean heart, O God. I know this means surrendering every corner of my life, every secret ambition, every hidden seductive temptation to Your searing, cleansing divine purity. O Lord, I do; forgive my hesitation.*

It is possible to talk a good talk even if we don't walk the walk, but not for long. Only people who yearn to be holy can talk about holiness. Let God's holiness burn through your soul until you stand surrendered—totally, unconditionally surrendered—before God almighty. Then out of that personal transformation, resolve to be a faithful example of holiness in a relativistic, promiscuous age.

Don't draw back from this task. Your decision will affect the future of the church, and the holy Creator of the galaxies will be your strength and shield.

# 4. Putting the Kingdom First

This little planet is a fantastic place full of incredible surprise and splendor. I hope you can rejoice in its goodness and beauty through travel, artistic expression, and meaningful employment. I hope you can enjoy the peace and security of never having to face the ravages of disease, famine, and war. I pray that you will know the happiness that comes from experiencing the material goodness of creation.

I also hope that you can experience the joy and happiness of Christian family. If you have chosen not to marry, I wish you a life of intimate pure friendship and the joy of extended family relations. If you have chosen to marry, I wish you a Christian marriage that lasts for a lifetime of ecstasy and pain, mistakes and growth, and steady progress in commitment and love. Personally, I would choose a lifetime of poverty rather than the agony of brokenness and divorce in marriage.

Spouse, family, material well-being, physical health—all of these forms of happiness are good. They are gifts from God. But they are finite, limited, partial. You and I are made to find ultimate meaning and happiness only as we walk humbly and obediently with our almighty Father. You and I are made to live forever in the presence of the Lord of the universe. The joy of that relationship far exceeds every earthly happiness.

That's why Jesus said: "Seek ye first the kingdom of God, and his righteousness; and all these things shall be added unto you" (Matt. 6:33, KJV). I see three important things about the kingdom of God in this text.

### How Happiness Comes

The first is a paradox. You cannot get happiness by aiming at it. Happiness comes only as a by-product when you aim at something else. If you aim at material happiness and make wealth your idol, you will get the gnawing emptiness of the rich person who constantly tears down and builds new barns in an ever more frantic search for security and satisfaction in things. If you aim at sexual happiness and make sexual thrills your idol, you will get loneliness, divorce, the suicide of a Marilyn Monroe, or the death by AIDS of a Rock Hudson.

Graham Kerr is a personal friend who formerly sought happiness in possessions, fame, and adulterous thrills. He became the host of an internationally famous TV program called the *Galloping Gourmet*. At the peak of his success, his show was the most widely watched TV program in history. Graham had all the happiness that a millionaire's money could buy—fancy cars, splendid houses, wine, women, and song. And he was miserable. At the height of all his "happiness," Graham's life was a shambles. He was an alcoholic and his marriage was a disaster.

One day, a maid in their home said to Treena, Graham's wife, "I know what could change your life. Come to church with me on Sunday." Treena was desperate so she went. That Sunday morning, she met Jesus Christ and her life was transformed. Graham was not interested in his wife's new religious ideas at first, but he watched her new behavior and joy. Three months later he decided that whatever had happened to Treena was good enough for him. He too accepted Christ as Lord and Savior. No longer did Graham aim at happiness through fame, money, and sex.

Since then, Graham's and Treena's lives have been radically changed. Christ and His kingdom come first for them. Graham stopped his syndicated TV program. They gave away their millions. They now live a simple lifestyle and serve in Christian ministry. They care about evangelism and the poor. They don't have many of the things they used to have, although they still have enough. One needs to spend only a little time with them to see the fantastic joy in their marriage. Together they have an excitement in Christian ministry that transcends the thrill of top Nielsen ratings for TV audiences.

Graham and Treena Kerr have truly put the kingdom first in their lives. Christ is Lord; therefore, they seek to live all the righteousness of family life, justice, and care for the poor that God desires. By aiming at the kingdom and its righteousness, they have also found happiness—the deep, abiding happiness of a dynamic walk with God, the secure happiness of Christian marriage, and the satisfying happiness that comes from possessing all the good gifts of the earth.

Putting God's kingdom first puts everything else in just the right place. The almighty Designer knows how everything fits together. So if we follow God's way for our lives, then we get everything right—our relationship with God, with neighbor, and with the earth. That's why Jesus said that if we seek first the kingdom, we will have everything else we need as a by-product.

Saint Augustine wrote that all of creation is a wedding ring from our Beloved. Material things are like a wonderful ring given to you and me by our divine Lover, God almighty. God wants us to enjoy them. But never forget the Beloved who gave them. If your fiancé gives you a special ring, he wants you to enjoy it. Imagine how silly it would be to forget your fiancé and think only of the ring. If we concentrate on the gift and forget the Giver, then we lose even the happiness God wants us to receive from the gift. Only when we put God first and do not look for happiness through created things will we receive even that happiness as a by-product.

Don't let anybody tell you that God does not want you to be happy. God wants you to dance with joy over the happiness of a loving family, a fulfilling job, a good house, enough food and money for daily needs, and some left over for special occasions. God would not have filled every little nook of creation with such gorgeous color and surprising splendor if He had not intended you and me to discover happiness in earthly things. But you cannot find happiness if you aim at it directly. It comes incidentally when you put God's kingdom first.

Jesus' promise that we will be happy if we put the kingdom first does not mean we will avoid trouble, danger, and struggle. Satan stalks the earth, seeking to destroy all the goodness God has created. Putting the kingdom first means defying Satan and all who obey him, and that can be costly. But even then, we can know a deep, abiding happiness in following Christ through the toughest times.

I had an uncle named Walter Winger, one of those Wingers whose Mennonite ancestors go back to the sixteenth-century Swiss Anabaptists in the Wenger Alps. Back then, when they put the kingdom first, they got hunted like animals, drowned in the rivers, and burned at the stake. Uncle Walter was an early missionary to Africa. That was a tough, painful, lonely calling. But he rejoiced in the ministry that God had given him. I remember him as an old man full of energy and the joy of God. Do you know what his favorite biblical text was? Matthew 6:33: "Seek ye first the kingdom of God, and his righteousness; and all these things shall be added unto you." He quoted Matthew 6:33 so often with so much confidence in its truth that even today, decades later, I still think of Matthew 6:33 as Uncle Walter's verse.

Kevin King is a Mennonite farm boy who has put the kingdom first. He wanted to raise a family on a Pennsylvania farm, but God called him to be a volunteer with Mennonite Central Committee

(MCC) in Brazil. So he lived for a time in a desperately poor village in the poorest section of southeast Brazil, helping malnourished peasants learn how to build a dam and grow better corn. I used to have an MCC poster on my wall that pictured Kevin and a poor Brazilian farmer looking proudly at that first tall crop of corn. A quiet happiness in Kevin's face proves that even when putting the kingdom first means separation from one's family, risk of tropical disease, and living on thirty-five dollars a month, Jesus' promise is still true. When we put the kingdom first, we get wonderful, deep, abiding happiness in the process.

### *Challenging the Status Quo*

A second important truth comes from Jesus' teaching about the kingdom. Jesus' kingdom challenges the *status quo* at every point it is wrong.

Jesus must have infuriated the Jewish men of His day. They were happy with the easy divorce laws that allowed them to get rid of their wives on almost any pretext. Jesus said no. He said God's way is for one man and one woman to live in lifelong covenant. The Jewish men of Jesus' day also considered women to be inferior. They would not appear in public with women. They said it was better to burn a copy of the Old Testament than give it to a woman. There was even a prayer that Jewish males of Jesus' day prayed: "I thank God I am not a Gentile, a slave, or a woman." Jesus totally rejected that male prejudice. He appeared with women in public. He discussed theology with women. He honored them with the first Resurrection appearance (even though the testimony of a woman had no weight in court!). Jesus said God's way, the kingdom's way, means equal dignity and respect for all.

Jesus also upset the rulers of His day. They loved to lord it over their subjects and pretend that oppression was for the good of everyone. Jesus said no. He said leaders should be servants if they want to follow kingdom values.

And Jesus terrified the economic establishment. He was constantly talking about sharing with the poor. He insisted that we should loan to the poor, even if there is no hope of repayment. As if that was not enough, He said in Matthew 25 that those who do not feed the hungry and clothe the naked go to hell. God's way, the kingdom's way, includes a costly concern for the poor and the weak.

Perhaps most radical of all, Jesus said the normal human way of attempting to guarantee our security through violence is wrong. Humanity has always sought peace and justice through the sword. Jesus said no. He called on His followers to love even their enemies and show the world the kingdom's new way to peace.

Well, you can see why Jesus was not too popular with the supporters of the *status quo*. The values of Jesus' kingdom so sharply challenged people who lived according to the *status quo* that they either had to change the way they lived or get rid of Jesus. They chose to kill Him rather than put the kingdom first.

Jesus' kingdom still challenges our world today in the same pointed way. Our world is crazy, even though its ways often look enticing.

Think of family life. Instead of being the centers of love and security God intended, our homes are often hell on earth. Half of American marriages dissolve in divorce. Millions of kids watch their parents fight and feud, ripping each other and their families to shreds.

Some time ago the choir of a Christian high school sang at our church. One song was a beautiful piece written by their director Clyde Hollinger. It was called "You Don't Have to Fear the Storm." He wrote it for his little son who was terrified one stormy summer evening by the crack and roar of thunder. In the song, Clyde tells how he took his little boy in his arms, held him real tight, and said softly, "Son, you don't have to fear the storm. I will be here with you all the time; you can trust my word."

Half the fathers and mothers today cannot honestly sing that song. You cannot honestly promise always to be there if you are going to end your marriage covenant and seek divorce when the going gets tough.

Do you believe Jesus knew what He was talking about? Do you intend to put His kingdom and its righteousness first in your life? If you do, then you must look this crazy society straight in the eye and say, "No! I refuse your stupid sexual values. I'll be faithful to my spouse. I'll make a marriage promise before God almighty that I will keep all my life, for better or for worse, in pain and in joy." I promise you that will sometimes be tough. I promise you that living the kingdom way will require a stubborn determination to defy the status quo that our society makes so attractive. And I can also promise you—on the authority of the One who sculpted the Rocky Mountains and set the stars in place, and on the basis of my own experience of many years of marriage—that Jesus' way on marriage is the way to deep, abiding, lifelong happiness.

Jesus' kingdom challenges the economic *status quo* in exactly the same way. More and more often today, our society says that happiness comes from money and big houses, limousines and luxuries that wealth can purchase. Our brightest and best youth go after the big money that buys trendy vacations, fashionable clothes, and meals at the best restaurants.

More and more Christians are buying that vision of the good life, trying to purchase the materialistic path to happiness. Is that really what you want to do with your life? Do you want to devote your life to worshiping expensive gadgets, costly perfumes, and ever more luxurious things at a time when millions starve and more than one billion have never once heard the Good News of Jesus' love for them?

The question is simple: *Do you really believe Jesus?* Do you believe what He said about sharing your life with the poor? Will you build bigger and bigger barns for yourself while Lazarus starves at the door?

I beg you to put the kingdom of God first. I beg you to join hundreds of other Christian volunteers linking arms with the poor in Brazil and Bangladesh, Peru and the Philippines, inner-city Los Angeles and Chicago. I beg you to join Uncle Walter and the hundreds of thousands who have left comfort and security to tell a dying world of the love of Jesus. I beg you to create a successful farm, a professional career, or a productive business whose daily practices and financial resources are totally surrendered to Christ and the work of His kingdom.

If you put the kingdom first in the financial area of your life, you will have to defy the *status quo* just as surely as in the area of sex and marriage. It will often be tough and costly. But here too I can promise you—on the authority of the One who created all the wealth of our fabulous planet and billions of others as well—that putting the kingdom first in your financial choices is the way to abiding happiness.

## *Influencing the World*

Third, this scripture passage tells us that if we put the kingdom first, we can take the values of Jesus' kingdom into every corner of life. I think this generation of Christians has a historic opportunity to do that.

Sometimes we Christians understand "separation from the world" in a way that erects big barriers between ourselves and the rest of society. We Anabaptists are especially guilty of this. We have often misunderstood "separation" as withdrawal from the world rather than separation from the sin of the world. So we withdrew to the countryside, wore our plain clothes, and had little to do with others except what was necessary to be successful farmers. We allowed ourselves little opportunity to share Jesus' kingdom principles with other people.

When I finished grade eight, I still parted my hair in the middle and I had never worn a necktie. I'll never forget the agony I experienced in my first few weeks of high school at Niagara Christian College. I had always parted my hair in the middle, but that summer before grade nine I got a brush cut. As my hair grew longer, I wanted desperately to part it on the side, but I thought that might be sin. So I prayed and struggled and kept combing it straight forward in order to postpone the final hour of decision. Finally, after far more anguish than you can imagine, I combed it to the side. One big step for Ron Sider! One small step for correcting our misunderstanding that separation from the sin of the world means last century's hairstyles and cultural withdrawal.

Other wings of the evangelical community had their own ways of withdrawing from the rest of society, but all that has changed. That is why this generation of evangelicals faces fantastic new opportunity—and also a new danger.

We are no longer withdrawn from the mainstream of society. We are doctors, nurses, and dentists, carpenters and plumbers, business leaders and professors, politicians and artists, working right in the center of the community. We have a historic opportunity to take the vision of Jesus' kingdom and apply it in the world of business or art, music or law, drama or medicine—whatever our chosen field.

This is God's world, even though sin has blown through it like a raging hurricane. God is about the business of restoring the broken beauty of His creation to the glory and wholeness He originally intended. That's what the good news of the kingdom is all about. Christians believe that, in spite of the power of evil all around, it is possible to live faithfully for God. Now by God's grace it is possible to reject adultery and live the kingdom's teaching on lifelong marriage; it is possible now to reject war and live the kingdom's way of reconciliation and peace; it is possible to run our businesses honestly and justly and share our wealth with the poor, the way Jesus did. It is possible now to reject the brokenness of modern filmmaking, art, music, law, and medicine and do all these things in a way that shouts to the world that the way of God's kingdom is a better way.

I hope that this generation of Christians will rise to meet this fantastic opportunity. We can transform education, health care, law, culture—and, yes, even politics—so that all these areas of society look a little more like the kingdom that Jesus announced.

What's the danger? Our temptation is no longer to withdraw from the world. Our greatest temptation today is to conform to the sin of society. As you and I plunge into the center of modern life, we experience powerful temptations to do things the way Hollywood and Wall Street and the Pentagon do things rather than the way Jesus did.

Only if we cling to a biblical understanding of separation from the world's sin can we Christians make a difference as we plunge into the center of modern society. The last thing our sad world needs is a few more people echoing the broken ideas of this self-centered materialistic society, ready to self-destruct in ethnic violence.

We can change our world *only* if we continue to believe and live the very different values of Jesus' kingdom. If you can model a joyful, loving family and a lifelong marriage covenant right in the middle of today's sexual wilderness and marital agony, you will change our world. If you can model Jesus' costly concern for justice for the poor in the midst of uncaring affluence and selfish materialism, you will change our world. If you dare to live Jesus' way of love for enemies in a costly challenge to nationalistic militarism and ethnic hatred, you will change our world.

What a fantastic opportunity! What a tremendous challenge! But you will never get started on this task of transformation unless you realize that the values of God's kingdom are radically different from the values of modern society. If you remember that, and if you resolve to put the kingdom ahead of everything else—ahead of money and status, ahead of security and convenience, ahead of power and nationalism—you will glorify the King of Kings. And in the process, you will have the time of your life.

# 5. Staying Married in a Crazy World

Christian marriage is the best gift that God has given me after himself. Throughout the Bible, God uses language borrowed from married life to talk about His intimate, personal relationship with you and me.

In the Old Testament, God said He was married to Israel. Israel was His virgin, His bride, His wife. In the New Testament, Jesus performed His first recorded miracle at the marriage in Cana. Paul said that the church is the bride of Christ. Then Revelation 19:9 gives us a picture of the final hope for which we yearn. And what is it? It is the marriage supper of the Lamb.

It is not an accident that the Bible frequently uses marriage language to talk about the personal relationship between God and His people. Both relationships are intimate, intended for boundless joy, happiness, and ecstasy. According to the Bible, the best clue about what it means to have a deep personal relationship with God comes from looking at the joy and the love shared by happily married couples. That is how special marriage is.

But every marriage experiences pain as well as joy. In the best of marriages there are storms, even occasionally seasons of storms when one tornado after another seems to tear through our lives. If the storms are not too frequent, if God is good, if we work at it, we can clean up our fields and our forests. We can clean up our marriages. The storms can be occasions for real growth, for deepening love, for the maturing of the relationship. Yet increasingly today, devastating moral hurricanes roar through marriages, ripping them apart. Even in the church, divorce is an ever more frequent reality.

Lifelong marriage is perhaps harder than in past generations. Our culture no longer supports marriage the way it once did. We no longer live in stable communities where lifelong marriage is the obvious, expected model for couples. Movies and television say marriage will not last. They show us that extramarital affairs are the norm. Pop psychology tells us that we should think only of ourselves, that we ought to be meeting our own needs, that we have a right to self-fulfillment. If a spouse is not meeting our needs, then of course we need to find somebody else who will. If we do not do that, we are not being true to ourselves. We owe it to ourselves to be fulfilled. Our society is crazy; it is messed up; it is falling apart at the point of the family.

We need to weep with those who have failed. God have mercy on us if we who still are married become proud, self-righteous, and judgmental. If we are honest, we know very well that we all face the same temptations, that we have walked close to the precipice. But we need not despair. Christian faith has the resources to restore the family and the joy of lifelong marriage covenant.

We can keep lifelong marriage covenants today if we understand and grasp firmly the three C's of Christian marriage: covenant, Cross, and church.

## The Covenant of Christian Marriage

First of all, let's think about the *covenant*. What is the biblical understanding of covenant? Genesis 2 and Matthew 19 help us understand. Genesis 2 is a marvelous story. Adam was not satisfied with the plants and the animals God had made, so God brought him Eve, who was bone of his bone and flesh of his flesh. Adam said, "Wow! That is what I have been looking for!" The man and the woman became one flesh. They became one permanently.

In Matthew 19, as Jesus dealt with the question of divorce, He quoted Genesis 2:24 and said that the two marriage partners become "one flesh" (v. 5). And then Jesus stated, "What God has joined together, let no one separate" (v. 6). Let no person end this divinely established covenant of unity for life. Jesus was saying that marriage is a lifelong commitment.

The best protection against giving up on marriage when there is pain (and there will always be pain in our marriages at some time or other) is to be committed without reservation for the rest of one's life. If that is clear, then we will struggle, we will cry, we will pray, and God will bring us through.

What then is a Christian marriage covenant? First of all, it is made before God—"what God has joined together." It is also made for life—"let no one separate." And it is to be made, you can be sure, with another believer. Only Christians can make that kind of lifelong promise with the assurance that God will bring them through.

Sometimes today people talk about a contractual marriage. They agree on what each party will do. If one party breaks the agreement and fails to keep the promises, then it is okay to dissolve the marriage because it was merely another human contract. Often the contract is implicit. We say, "Let us try it. Let us see if it works. Let us see if it feels good. Let us see if it meets my needs." In all that, of course, the hidden assumption of contract is that each partner has a right to self-fulfillment. "If I am not getting my needs met, then the contract is off," we say. "If my spouse does not meet my needs, then the contract is broken."

This is not the Christian marriage covenant. It is the devil's cheap substitute. It is a fraud. It is a trick, although Satan beguiles us with the idea that it brings freedom. He says a contractual marriage brings liberation. He says, "Society changes; you change. How on earth can you make a lifelong covenant?"

I want to shout to all of us: "Let us not be deceived by Satan's substitute!" Let us choose an unconditional solemn covenant before God rather than a limited liability contract. In God's name, let us choose partners who will walk with us in a lifelong marriage covenant. That is the only foundation strong enough to bring us to the deep joy of fiftieth wedding anniversaries and beyond. Covenant, biblical covenant before God, is the first *C* of Christian marriage.

### *The Cross of Christian Marriage*

The second *C* of Christian marriage is the *Cross*. Anybody who has been married for even a few weeks knows that there is pain as well as joy in marriage. Each of us is a proud, selfish, petty, silly sinner. We hurt each other and then, silly as we are, we try to cover it up or we try to blame the other person. We refuse to say we are sorry. It happens in the best of marriages. There is only one solution to all of that. It is a difficult solution. It is the solution at the heart of the gospel. It is the Cross—costly forgiveness.

We learn from Ephesians 5 that we are supposed to love our wives (I think it applies to wives as well as husbands) as Christ loved the church. How did Christ love the church? He died for it. He went to the cross. Why? Because you and I are such miserable sinners. That is why. Every marriage has that kind of pain. Every marriage needs that kind of forgiveness.

The second *C* of Christian marriage—the Cross, costly forgiveness—is closely related to the first *C*, covenant. The Cross means never giving up. As long as we live, Christ stands there offering us forgiveness, repentance. God does not say, "I have had enough of you. I have had enough of your stupidity, of your silliness, of your unfaithfulness, of your sin and your failures." He continually says, "I will give you another chance."

Taking the way of the Cross in our marriages, loving our spouses as Christ loved the church, means never giving up, even in a difficult, painful time. It is the only way to healing and to joy. It is the only way to happiness in marriage. Pain and failure will always come, even in the best of marriages. The only way to restoration and joy is costly forgiveness.

### *The Church of Christian Marriage*

The third C is the *church*. Young people may say, "All this sounds kind of scary. The demands seem very high. Lifelong commitment is a hard calling." You are right; it is. But remember, we are not alone. The risen Christ is in us. We have the power of God to keep our promises, and we also have the love and support of the church. All of the other brothers and sisters in the body of Christ promise to help us, and that is why we have church weddings rather than just going off by ourselves to elope. The wedding covenant is not just a solemn covenant between God and two persons; it is also a solemn covenant in front of our Christian brothers and sisters. They all promise, by attending the wedding, to help us in that marriage covenant. Notice how Paul quotes Genesis 2 in Ephesians 5:29–32:

> For no one ever hates his own body, but he nourishes and tenderly cares for it, just as Christ does for the church, because we are members of his body. "For this reason a man will leave his father and mother and be joined to his wife, and the two will become one flesh." This is a great mystery, and I am applying it to Christ and the church.

Paul says that becoming one flesh in marriage is symbolic in some way of Christ's union with the church. Notice he says it symbolizes the union between Christ and *the church*, not the union between Christ and the individual Christian. We do not serve Christ as individual Christians. We are part of His Body. We are all united in the church with Christ, our Bridegroom. That makes us one. As Paul wrote in 1 Corinthians 12:26, if one suffers, we all suffer; if one rejoices, we all rejoice. That is why we come together in the body of Christ to celebrate a wedding or an anniversary.

The other side of this truth is that we stand together when there are tough times. That is what we promise every young couple who comes to be married in the church: We are responsible for each other's marriages. Everybody in a congregation is responsible if someone's marriage fails. Did we pray or gossip? Did we cry or silently sneer? Did we gently counsel them to hold on, or did we stay coldly silent?

There are lots of ways that this third C, the church, is crucial today. We need much more of an emphasis on teaching our young people the beauty and joy and lifelong commitment of Christian marriage. We need more premarital counseling. I wish we would say in our churches that we will not solemnize the marriage of a man and a woman unless they have gone through several months of Christian marriage counseling. We need better counseling during marriage, too. We need to tell each other it is okay to seek counseling if we are having struggles in our marriage.

Some Christians are too proud to do that. I think God has given Arbutus and me one of the best marriages I have seen, but as I noted earlier, there came a time when we very badly needed counseling. I was too proud to do that for quite a while. I knew that many marriages around us were in trouble and that they needed help. In fact, I encouraged some of those couples to get counseling. But me? Not me. Thank God, after awhile when I hurt enough, I was ready to get help. Six months of marriage counseling for Arbutus and me with a wonderful Christian counselor was a tremendously important healing experience for us.

Marriage Encounter is another way that the church can strengthen marriages. Couples come together for a weekend to learn new techniques for tasting each other's feelings and for understanding each other. After Arbutus and I attended a session, we could pray as if we were standing in each other's shoes.

Satan is a clever liar. He says marriages used to last because people had no other option. They hated each other and they lived parallel lives, but they stayed together just because of custom. That is partly true and partly a lie, but the church gives us a way of handling the truth in this charge. I am not saying we should live forever in a terrible marriage, merely enduring the agony. However, there are ways to work at the pain, the failures, the hurts in each of our marriages. The church can and must help us do that.

If your marriage is in trouble, share your pain with your pastor or with a Christian marriage counselor. Go to a Marriage Encounter weekend. Discover through the support of your church that forgiveness, healing, renewal are possible in your marriage. The body of Christ, the church, is the support given by God for your lifelong marriage covenant.

Covenant, Cross, and church are absolutely essential for Christian marriage today. If we resolve as a church to strengthen Christian marriage in the body of Christ, then we can promise our children and grandchildren that they can reach the joyous landmark of a fiftieth wedding anniversary filled with the mature love that comes when one man and one woman walk together through the joy and pain of life, loving and crying together, forgiving and rejoicing, forgetting and exulting together. We can all look forward, thank God, to that final marriage celebration when we will gather together to sing and rejoice at the marriage supper of the Lamb.

# 6. In Word and Deed

A dear friend of mine named Dennis is now a Mennonite pastor in the city of Philadelphia. About thirty years ago, Brother Dennis was an angry black militant who hated white people. He once told me that if he had met me back then, he might have killed me. I'm glad he met Jesus first!

Before that happened, his life was disintegrating. He was abusing alcohol, his marriage was falling apart, and he landed in prison for committing a major crime. In prison, Dennis read the Bible. Eventually, he opened his heart to Christ and became a Christian.

He came out, struggled a bit, and then the pastor at Diamond Street Mennonite Church in Philadelphia discipled him and the Lord put his life back together. It's a tremendous story of renewal. Dennis's marriage was restored. He got a decent job. He owns his own home. He is now pastoring a small Mennonite congregation on a part-time basis.

Anybody who thinks that Brother Dennis simply needed a better welfare system, a better job training program, or whatever really doesn't understand his problem. He needed a radical transformation at the core of his being. That happened as he came to a living faith in Christ and the Holy Spirit slowly transformed him. At the same time, anybody who thinks that Dennis's problems were solved once he accepted Christ and was born again—even though the schools did not work for his children and he couldn't get a job and couldn't buy a house—doesn't understand his predicament, either. He needed all of those things as well as the transformation of his heart.

It puzzles me why people who worship the eternal Word-become-flesh have torn apart word and deed, as we have in the Christian church. But it has happened in astonishing ways. Let me share two stories out of my life experience.

In 1979, I was in South Africa for about two weeks to attend a major event called SACLA, which pulled together about five thousand people from all the nation's denominations and races. In the preceding week, before I spoke to that group, I attended an annual meeting of a white evangelical university movement. This Christian group had been divided, like the rest of the country, into white English-speaking, white Afrikaans-speaking, colored, and black segments. I delivered addresses to the white English-speaking group in which I talked about Jesus' resurrection and God's concern for the poor.

I got to know a young man at these meetings (let's call him James) who was not a Christian. He was Jewish. But James was intrigued by the vital Christian faith of these white evangelical kids, so he came to the conference. I learned that he was deeply involved in the struggle against apartheid. He was fervently committed to social justice in his country. In fact, he was trying to be a full-time student and a full-time activist. He gave me a great political education.

One evening, after a three-hour conversation, James said to me, "Ron, I'm burned out." I wasn't surprised, considering all he was trying to do. But then he said something that really startled me: "Ron, God told me that if I would come to this conference, I would learn something about His Son."

You can imagine my surprise because I knew he was Jewish. I said, "James, I believe that Jesus died on the cross for your sins. I believe that He rose on the third day for you."

He said, "I believe all of that. I really do." Yet something held him back from becoming a Christian, and he immediately told me what it was. "I don't want to be like these white Christians here," he said. "They sing about heaven. They talk about the joy of Jesus. But they don't care about justice in South Africa."

He thought that coming to personal faith in Jesus Christ would mean losing his commitment to the struggle against apartheid. I said, "Goodness, no, James! Jesus wants to strengthen that commitment in you. He doesn't want to take it away. Salvation will have to be on His terms, of course, but it will involve a deeper commitment than ever."

I did not want to hurry him along because sometimes we Christians get too pushy at this point. (Actually, 99 percent of the time, we are too hesitant!) But I said, "If you'd like to pray, I'd be happy to do that with you."

He said, "Let's do."

We went to my room and he prayed a beautiful prayer, confessing his sins and accepting Jesus Christ as his Lord and Savior. I prayed, too. When we were finished, I looked at James and his face was shining. After he left, I was so excited that all I could do was walk around the room, singing praises to the Lord. I wish that sort of thing would happen every week in my life. (Pray for me in that regard.)

Think about what my conversation with James tells us about the division in today's church. You can be sure that those white evangelical kids had invited him to Jesus many, many times, but he couldn't hear their invitation because they didn't care about justice in their society.

Now let me share my second story: A couple of years later, I was asked to be one of the speakers at the thirtieth anniversary of the founding of the National Council of Churches (NCC) in the United States. I was delighted to go. I looked at the roster of seminars and saw there were about a dozen on ecumenical affairs. I think that's an important subject, so I was pleased to see that. I saw about fifteen seminars on peace and justice; I was delighted with that. But I looked for seminars on evangelism and on cross-cultural sharing of the gospel. Do you know how many of those seminars there were? Absolutely zero.

Now those two snapshots don't give you totally accurate pictures of either the NCC or the evangelical church in South Africa, but they do point to an amazing one-sidedness in the Christian church. I want to challenge you to think about how we can overcome it.

### *What Evangelism Really Is*

Let me make one clarifying point, however. When I use the word *evangelism*, I don't mean the ghastly stereotype of evangelism done badly—i.e., people ramming tracts down prospects' throats, accosting folks on the streets, and so on. I'm not talking about any certain method. I'm talking about longing and praying for sensitive ways to invite people to confess Jesus Christ as their Lord and Savior. I'm talking about looking for positive ways to invite people into a living relationship with Christ and to join His new community.

Some congregations major on evangelism and don't seem at all concerned about the fact that hurting people live just a few miles away from them, in an inner city or on an Indian reservation. At the same time, other Christians talk a lot about social justice and work at peacemaking, but they never get around to inviting people who don't know Christ to meet Him. Both approaches are wrong. Both need to change.

Wayne Gordon grew up in the Midwest. (I believe it was a small town in Iowa.) He had a perfect Sunday school attendance record for six or seven years, but he had never personally opened his heart to Jesus Christ. He finally did that on an Athletes for Christ weekend outing, when he was a student in grade ten. After he returned home, Wayne lay on his bed, staring at the ceiling. He said, "God, I want You to know that I'll do anything You want me to do with my life. . . ." Almost immediately, he felt called to the inner city.

He woke his parents and said, "God has called me to work in the inner city, and I have to go."

They said, "Well, that's fine, Wayne. But it's probably best if you finish high school!"

He did that. He also finished college. Then he went to work in inner-city Chicago in a neighborhood where the infant mortality rates were approaching the levels found in developing nations. He began to love whole persons. He began to lead Bible studies and start recreational clubs and build housing. He set up a medical clinic, which now has twenty-one full-time doctors. The whole program of ministry has grown and grown, and Wayne's congregation is at the center of it.

It hasn't been easy. The night that Wayne and Ann came back from their honeymoon, someone broke into their apartment. They were burglarized nine more times in the next three years. But they persisted. They invited people to faith in Christ and worked at alleviating the social problems of that community. God has blessed them with a congregation of more than a thousand members and a budget of $10 million a year. Most of the people attending that church have come to personal faith in Jesus Christ through its many social programs. That's the kind of thing I have in mind when I speak of combining evangelism and social ministry.

I wonder what God would do with a few thousand people like Wayne Gordon, who would dare to look into the face of the Lord and say, "I'll do anything You want me to do with my life"? It would be interesting to know.

Why have we Christians torn apart word and deed? I think part of the problem is our theology. I want to look briefly at four areas where our theology has not been adequately biblical and, as a result, we have not effectively combined word and deed—evangelism and social ministry.

### Who People Really Are

First, let us consider our *doctrine of Creation,* the question of who people really are. The issue of Creation is much broader than that, of course, but let us focus on that aspect of it for a moment.

Our world has two misguided understandings of who people are. There is the secular view, which sees people as if they were complex machines. This view supposes that human beings are nothing more than sophisticated socioeconomic entities. It assumes that all we must do to change people is to change their environment. However, the Bible says we are spiritual beings as well as material beings.

The second view is a hyperspiritualized concept. The Greek philosopher Plato said that every person has a good soul, trapped in an evil body, so he believed the body is really not all that important; all that matters is the spiritual part. Many Christians have become rather Platonic in this regard. They are interested almost exclusively in "saving souls," but the Bible teaches that we are bodies and souls, *and* our entire beings matter to God.

According to the Bible, the human body is so good that the Creator chose to become human flesh. The body is so good that Jesus rose bodily from the dead. The body is so good that, when He returns, He promises to raise you and me bodily. Understanding that persons are body-soul unities, and that both sides of life are crucial, will help us in putting together word and deed.

### What the Gospel Really Is

The second theological issue is the *wholeness of the gospel*. Just what is the gospel? Some people would say, "It's the forgiveness of sins." Or to put it a bit more theologically, "It's justification by faith alone." But if the gospel promises merely the forgiveness of sins, then it's sort of like a one-way ticket to heaven, and we might assume that we can live like hell till we get there. We could conclude that we can accept the gospel, get forgiven, and go on being just as adulterous, just as materialistic, and just as racist as we were before because the gospel assures the forgiveness of our sins.

Others would say, "The gospel is the message of peace, and we spread the gospel by trying to end war." I wouldn't dispute that, but I don't think it is a complete picture of the gospel, either.

What did Jesus say the gospel is? Mark's summary of Jesus' whole preaching appears in these verses: "Now after John was arrested, Jesus came to Galilee, proclaiming the gospel of God, and saying, 'The time is fulfilled, and the kingdom of God has come near; repent, and believe in the gospel'" (1:14-15).

Almost every time Jesus talked about it, He described the *gospel* as the good news of the kingdom. That's not the kind of terminology we use in our everyday language on the street, however; so what did He mean by "the kingdom"?

The Jewish prophets had said long before, in a time of idolatry and oppression of the poor, that God would send foreign conquerors to wipe out the nations of Israel and Judah. They also said that the Messiah would come to bring a new right relationship with God, a new forgiveness of sins, and a new right relationship with one's neighbors—a time of *shalom* (peace). In God's new kingdom, the poor would be cared for.

Hundreds of years later, Jesus came along—quietly, cautiously, but with increasing clarity—claiming to be that Messiah. Remember the scene where the Pharisees accused Jesus of casting out demons by the power of Satan? Jesus rejected their accusation and insisted that He was casting out demons by the power of God. He said, "If it is by the finger of God that I cast out the demons, then the kingdom of God has come to you" (Luke 11: 20). The kingdom had already broken into human history. The messianic kingdom that the Jews were expecting had actually arrived, Jesus said, in His person and work.

There were two parts to this kingdom, just as the prophets had said: a vertical part (our relationship with God) and a horizontal part (our relationship with our neighbors). The vertical part is crucial. You don't get into Jesus' kingdom by joining Evangelicals for Social Action and working hard for peace and justice in the world, as important as that is. Zealots in Jesus' day thought that if they could get the whole Jewish nation to rise up in armed rebellion, the Messiah would come. The Pharisees thought that if all the Jews obeyed the Law perfectly for a day, the Messiah would come. Jesus said, no, both ideas were wrong. You get into this new kingdom by sheer grace because God loves to forgive prodigal sons and daughters. We can stand before a holy God only because Jesus died on the cross for our sins. So forgiveness of sins is at the center of the gospel. That's how we get into this new kingdom.

But there's also a horizontal aspect to the gospel. Jesus was not an isolated preacher who went around the country, whispering to isolated hermits, "Your sins are forgiven. . . . Your sins are forgiven. . . ." He formed a new community of people. He gathered a new circle of disciples. And their new social order was very different from the rest of society. They loved the whole person, and they challenged the status quo in all kinds of astonishing ways.

Think with me for a moment about the way Jesus' circle of disciples challenged society. For starters, they challenged the demons and cast them out. They challenged the rich. (Jesus said scandalous things about wealthy people.) They challenged the attitudes toward people with disabilities. (The Dead Sea Scrolls tell us that the Essene monastic community of Jesus' day would not allow disabled people in their assembly, but Jesus said that when His people gather together, they should especially invite people who cannot walk and people who cannot see.) They challenged the prevailing attitudes toward women. (Women were not even close to being considered equals with men in the first century. Jesus crashed through that male prejudice.)

Jesus said His followers should challenge the *status quo* by loving their enemies. That's probably the most radical thing of all that He said. Hardly anyone, before or since Jesus, has been able to live up to that. Even the church, for most of its history, has not really taken that statement seriously.

So when Jesus talked about the gospel, He meant both a horizontal and a vertical gospel. He meant that we can stand before a holy God only because Jesus died on the cross for our sins. He also meant that a new messianic kingdom is now breaking into history; there is a new society, a new community of people in whose midst everything is being transformed. That's good news. Christians can invite people into that new community.

One of the reasons the early church was so successful in its evangelism was that people could see this new community living the gospel. Christian men accepted women; Christian masters accepted slaves. Onlookers saw love expressed in the most remarkable ways in that group of people, and they said, "What on earth is going on here?" In response, the Christians told them about Jesus and invited them to faith.

Today, the church so often looks like the world that the question is not asked. Thus, we lose the opportunity to share our faith. We need to remember that the church itself is part of the Good News.

If the gospel is the good news of the kingdom, if that kingdom is actually becoming visible now in Jesus' new messianic circle (the church), and if that new community actually models Jesus' concern for the whole person and Jesus' concern for the poor—if all of these things are true—then it's impossible to embrace Jesus' gospel and do only evangelism or do only social ministry. They must go together.

### What Salvation Really Is

A third theological point has been distorted. That's the *doctrine of salvation.* If we gain a more biblical understanding of salvation, we will begin to understand that it means much more than evangelical Christianity often suggests. The individualistic, privatizing distortion that has happened with the gospel has also happened with our understanding of salvation. We have often reduced salvation to mean nothing more than "Jesus and me." We suppose it is merely Jesus' blessing of each believer's eccentric way. But if we study what the New Testament says about salvation, we'll see that's not true.

Salvation includes not just the forgiveness of my sins, but also the way that the Holy Spirit begins to sanctify me as I come into a living relationship with Christ. It doesn't stop there, either! Salvation includes the transforming relationships that arise within the circle of people who accept Christ.

The story of Zacchaeus is striking at this point. Zacchaeus was a wicked tax collector, caught in an unjust structure. He was using that structure for all it was worth. Then he came face-to-face with Jesus, and he gave back everything that he had taken wrongly. Moreover, he gave much of his money to caring for the poor. The final sentence in that story is this: "Jesus said to him, 'Today salvation has come to this house'" (Luke 19:9). Notice there's not a single word in the whole text about the forgiveness of sins. I'm sure that forgiveness happened. The rascal needed it, and I have no doubt that Jesus forgave his sins. But that's not what the Bible talks about here. It talks about the changed economic relationships that Zacchaeus had after he came to Jesus Christ. Salvation in the New Testament includes the new changed relationships in the body of Christ. Salvation involves not only my relationship with God, but also my relationship within the community of believers.

### *Who Jesus Really Is*

One more theological point: *The question of Jesus* is vital to the whole issue of evangelism and social ministry. Who is Jesus? A great ethical prophet? A noble peacemaker? From the time of the early church, Christians have said that He is more. Throughout the centuries, Christians have confessed with Peter that "there is no other name under heaven given among mortals by which we must be saved," except Jesus Christ (Acts 4:12). Jesus said, "I am the way, and the truth, and the life. No one comes to the Father except through me" (John 14:6).

You see, if Jesus was just a great prophet, then it would be blasphemy to worship Him and to say what Peter said. Furthermore, if Jesus was only a profound ethical teacher, then there's no particular urgency to invite people to accept Him. There are other great teachers.

But if, as the church has confessed throughout the ages, the carpenter from Nazareth is truly God in the flesh and the only way to the Father, then Christian evangelism is urgent business.

In the first century, Greeks believed that gods and goddesses appeared on earth with some regularity. Saul of Tarsus was no Greek polytheist. Jews were strict monotheists; they insisted there is only one God. Saul of Tarsus was the strictest of them, yet he said in Philippians 2 that "at the name of Jesus every knee should bend . . . and every tongue should confess that Jesus Christ is Lord" (vv. 10-11). (The Greek word here translated as *Lord* was also used in translating the Old Testament from Hebrew into Greek. Wherever the Hebrew word *Yahweh* appeared in the Old Testament, denoting the one God, the Greek Old Testament used the word *kurios*. So Paul said in Philippians 2 that the carpenter of Nazareth, Jesus, is *kurios*. He is the one God.)

If we believe what the New Testament says about Jesus, then we will want to share Him as rapidly, as eagerly, and as sensitively as we can. We must combine Christian word and deed. We must combine evangelism and social ministry. Let me tell you a couple of stories to illustrate how this works.

Wanda Caldwell was a sixteen-year-old when she came to a ministry very much like the one Wayne Gordon leads. It was based just a few miles away, in fact, and was a ministry of the same sort. In 1983, she got help at that ministry and went out into the streets again. She came back a year later. She needed surgery on her stomach, and the church arranged for it. The doctor even prayed with her before he operated.

She left again. She indulged in alcohol regularly. She ran up bills in ten different names and was behind payment on all of them. The law was beginning to catch up with her, and she was in despair, so she came back to the church a third time. The first person she met was the doctor who had prayed with her on the operating table. He welcomed her and the church invited her to be a part of its ministry.

Wanda couldn't believe the warmth of the welcome they offered her. She said, "It was like the Spirit of the Lord engulfed me and hugged me." They walked with her month after month as she struggled with what it means to truly follow Jesus. She said the people of the church had remarkable patience with her. If they had given up, she probably would have gone back out on the streets. But they kept telling Wanda that they loved her, although she didn't think she was worthy to be loved.

Today, she is off the welfare roll. She is a committed Christian. She sings in the choir. She is a transformed woman because of that ministry, which puts together word and deed.

Deer Valley Baptist Church in 1970 was a small congregation of about a hundred people. They were middle-class, satisfied folks living in a comfortable neighborhood of Denver, and they were trying to persuade a new pastor to come. One candidate said, "I'm only willing to come on one condition: You've got to get rid of all your committees." That was a pretty startling idea for a Baptist church, but they agreed.

The new pastor started preaching about God's special concern for the poor. He started talking more about social ministry, about evangelism, and about training people to do the work of the kingdom. He said they should unleash the laity, get out of their ecclesiastical fortress, and begin working in the world.

In the next twelve years, that congregation grew to one thousand members. They were doing evangelism everywhere. They started about a dozen ministries to the poor throughout the city of Denver. That's what I mean about combining word and deed.

I think that a proper understanding of key points of biblical theology will lead us to combine word and deed, to do evangelism and social ministry. This issue has taken on a new urgency in an interesting way because of new developments in American society.

For decades, the secular leadership of our nation tended to push religious people to the margin and rejected them. They thought that all they needed to do to solve social problems was to change the environment. They thought that if they got the economic incentives right, got the educational system right, and so on, society would be transformed. All of those things are important, but they are not enough.

In the past eight or ten years, there has been quite an astonishing change on the part of the intellectual elite who lead American society. They have a new openness to the role of religious faith, especially faith-based organizations.

In 1998, Rev. Eugene Rivers was on the cover of Newsweek magazine because he is an inner-city Boston pastor deeply engaged in evangelism and social ministry. As a result of the gang ministry that he and several other pastors were doing, the homicide rate in Boston had dropped to zero for twenty-seven months. Both Mr. Gore and Mr. Bush promised in the presidential election campaign of 2000 that, if they were elected president, they would put faith-based organizations at the center of their anti-poverty programs.

Why has this happened? Why this dramatic change of attitude?

Our nation tried liberal political solutions to overcoming poverty. Some worked and some didn't. Then we tried conservative political solutions, and those didn't end poverty. By the start of the new century, the policy elites in our government and our universities realized that we had a brokenness at the core of our great cities—evidenced by gang violence, drugs, and high out-of-wedlock birth rates. Our leaders felt moral outrage at this and they feared it was a threat to our democracy, but they didn't know what to do about it. When the late Senator Daniel P. Moynihan, who was at the center of our social policy in the United States for forty years, gave lectures on this subject at Harvard University, he said in conclusion, "We don't have a clue what sort of social policy would be adequate to change this."

Then evidence began to emerge about Christian ministries that were changing the core of our large cities. Secular leaders heard about ministry programs that were really working, dramatically successful programs.

For example, one sociological study of Teen Challenge found a success rate two or three times that of secular drug rehabilitation programs. The crucial difference in approach was Teen Challenge's commitment to share the gospel with people.

A Harvard economist tried to determine what sort of inner-city black male was most likely to escape the syndrome of drugs, violence, and poverty. He measured attendance at school, involvement in athletic activities, the effect of two-parent families, and other factors. He even included church attendance, though most of his colleagues didn't think that would make any difference. Guess what was the most important predictor of whether an inner-city kid would survive? It was church attendance.

Because this sort of evidence began emerging with more and more clarity, we have reached a moment in this nation that I would not have dared to predict ten years ago. Now prominent leaders in government, in the communications media, and in the academic world are saying to people of Christian faith, "You seem to know something that we don't, so go ahead. Take the lead. We're opening the door."

We Christians now have a historic opportunity for leadership in this nation, which we have not had for a long time. I'm not sure that the church is ready for it. Do we have enough churches that really understand how word and deed fit together, how evangelism and social action fit together? Too many church ministries to the poor are actually secular programs, run by Christians and perhaps located at a church building. Isn't that a little strange? If we Christians truly believe that people are spiritual beings as well as material beings, shouldn't we work at spiritual transformation at the same time we work at physical transformation?

## How to Combine Word and Deed

Let me make a few suggestions about what congregations might do in order to combine word and deed. First of all, take a careful audit of ministries and examine what they're really doing. How much evangelism is really going on? How much social ministry is really going on? Are those two aspects of ministry fitting together so that they complement each other? If you find that you're doing only one or the other, ask your church leaders, "Wouldn't we be more effective if we worked with the whole person instead of half the person? Doesn't that fit Jesus' teachings much better?"

Second, train your congregation's people to put word and deed together. In my book *Cup of Water, Bread of Life,* I share ten stories of ministries that are actually doing Christ's work in both word and deed. I found that the two aspects of Christian ministry fit together only if the evangelism is intentional, only if the local leaders understand that evangelism is crucial, and then train the people doing social ministry in how to lead someone to Christ.

Wayne Gordon's favorite phrase for the kind of evangelism he does is "friendship evangelism" or "relational evangelism." It comes out of the relationships that slowly develop as you get to know people and respect them as whole persons.

Third, start small. Ichthus Fellowship in London is one of the stories I tell in that earlier book. It started with about fifteen people in a poor neighborhood. It's now a ministry of about two thousand persons. One of the things they did in the early years was called Jesus Action. They posted little signs around the neighborhood that simply said, "Jesus Action: Need Help? Call . . . ," and then gave the church's phone number. A few people from the congregation were willing to donate their time each week to answer the phones and see how they could meet these needs.

Roger and Faith Forrester are the two key pastors in that ministry. Faith told me that she was answering the phone when a call came from a woman who said, "I saw your sign. I want the action, but I don't want Jesus. I don't want anybody ramming religion down my throat."

Faith said, "We don't do that here. What can I do to help you?"

She spent two or three hours with the woman, helping her get groceries and doing a variety of things. When they were finished, they sat down in the woman's living room. The lady gave Faith some tea. Almost immediately, the woman asked, "Now what's this about Jesus?"

"But I promised not to talk about that," Faith replied.

The woman smiled and said, "C'mon." So they talked about Jesus.

In another case, they helped a grandmother whose apartment had been flooded. A couple of days later, the granddaughter called and asked, "Are you the people who dried out Grammy?"

When they said yes, the young woman blurted out, "I'd like to be a Christian."

The conversations didn't typically go that way, believe me. They usually involved a much longer relationship. But the members of Ichthus Fellowship learned that they could start small.

Finally, collect the successful stories of ministry. Find models that are analogous to your situation, and learn from them. In Evangelicals for Social Action, we have a ministry called Network 935 because Matthew 9:35 says that Jesus went about preaching, teaching, and healing—in other words, combining word and deed. Network 935 involves an Internet Web site and other forms of communications to help churches put together evangelism and social ministry in a way that's sensitive and relational. We share true stories of how churches are doing it. I'm convinced that any congregation can move toward a deeper combination of word and deed if the people catch a vision for it.

Vinay and Colleen Samuel, a couple of my close friends, are middle-class Indian Christians. Vinay did doctoral studies at Cambridge University in England. After a few years, he returned to Bangalore and became the pastor of the most prestigious Anglican church there. It was a growing congregation, and things were going well.

However, Vinay and Colleen became dissatisfied because they weren't ministering enough to hurting, poor people. So they started a little school under a tree for kids who didn't have enough money to buy the uniforms to go to regular schools. Then they discovered that some of the young girls were being sold into prostitution because their parents were desperately poor, so they started an orphanage for them. They started making microloans to people in the community. The ministry made literally hundreds of loans to start small businesses there. On and on it went. Today, that ministry in Bangalore serves fifty thousand people every year.

The Samuels had to be very sensitive to their culture in India. The relationship between Hindus, Muslims, and Christians there is delicate. But these Christians carefully share the gospel and a number of congregations have developed out of their ministry.

One day, a woman named Lola walked into the back of one of those small congregations. Lola was the most famous prostitute in all of Bangalore. She controlled twenty-five thousand prostitutes and could swing elections with their votes. Nobody tangled with her. She was widely feared, so when she walked into the back of that church, a wave of terror swept through the congregation, but Colleen is absolutely fearless. She walked over and put her arm around her. "Lola," she said, "I'm so glad you're here!" And Lola began coming to church.

After attending church for six months, Lola accepted Jesus Christ as her Lord and Savior. Vinay and Colleen discipled her as the Holy Spirit transformed her. At the end of two years, she said, "I want to be baptized."

They had baptized many Hindus and Muslims before, but this case was different. Lola was probably the most famous Muslim woman in Bangalore. They knew that if they baptized her, religious riots could erupt and their whole ministry might be wiped out.

So Vinay did something very unusual. He went to the local Muslim leader, the imam, and said, "My friend Lola wants to be baptized. Why don't you try to persuade her not to be a Christian?" The imam's jaw dropped.

"Yes," Vinay said, "take a whole month."

Just three days later, the imam came knocking on Vinay's door. He said, "I can't do a thing with her. She's so much better off with you."

"Well, does that mean it's okay for me to baptize her?" Vinay asked.

The imam shrugged his shoulders and said, "Do what you like."

Vinay baptized her. There were no riots. Today, Lola is a full-time evangelist with that church.

That's what I mean by combining word and deed, integrating evangelism and social ministry. Lola knew about all of the social ministries of the church when she walked into the back of that little congregation. That's why she wanted to hear the gospel.

Christians today need to recover what the Anabaptists knew in the sixteenth century when they began putting together word and deed in powerful ways. God can still use us to bind up hurting people, lead them to personal faith in Christ, transform our society, and glorify our Lord.

# 7. If Christ Is Not Risen

Picture yourself listening as Peter and the other apostles talk sadly on the Friday night after the Crucifixion. They talk about Jesus' amazing life and miracles. They talk about the way they had slowly come to believe that Jesus was the long-expected Jewish Messiah who would drive out the foreign conquerors and finally bring their nation freedom. They talk about the intense excitement of the previous week, when the crowds waved palm branches and gladly cheered Jesus as the Messiah.

But now Jesus is dead, finished. They all know what the Law says: "Cursed is everyone who hangs on a tree" (Gal. 3:13). The religious leaders had never accepted Jesus' breathtaking claims to be the Messiah, the Son of God, and now they had convicted Him of blasphemy and had arranged for Him to be killed to prove that Jesus was a false prophet. Jesus' desperately discouraged disciples drew the only possible conclusion: Jesus was finished. Their soaring hopes in Him were shredded. Jesus was not the Messiah; He was not the unique Son of God. He was a false messianic pretender. That was the proper conclusion on that awful Friday evening.

That would have been the proper conclusion forever, except for one thing. Three days later, on Easter morning, the same discouraged disciples later would tell us, the carpenter from Nazareth burst from the tomb, leaving nothing behind but a little pile of grave clothes. He appeared to His frightened disciples, assuring them that He was alive forevermore. He walked, talked, and ate with them to dispel their doubts. He explained to them that He was the Messiah (though not the warlike military hero that so many Jews of the time were expecting) and He promised to return someday to complete His victory over sin, injustice, and evil, resurrecting all those who believe in Him.

The New Testament records a fantastic change wrought by Jesus' resurrection. The Resurrection and Pentecost transformed frightened men and women into bold, daring preachers and missionaries who risked their lives to crisscross the Roman Empire, telling anybody who would listen that Jesus the Messiah had risen from the dead.

But is that true? That's what they said, but can intelligent, thinking people in the modern world really believe that?

For many modern intellectuals, the answer to that question is very clear. The answer is no. These intellectuals think that modern science has made it impossible to accept miracles as real historical events that actually happened. They point out that modern science has explained more and more of the things that people in earlier ages used to explain as miracles. They conclude that, eventually, science will be able to explain everything. Nothing, they suppose, exists except the natural order around us that science so logically describes, predicts, and explains. Alleged miracles are just imaginary stories that naïve folk used to tell before they knew how things really worked. So Jesus' resurrection didn't really happen, although maybe we can still use the word *resurrection*. The disciples must have made up the story, or perhaps they had hallucinations. That's what most secular intellectuals in our great universities think today.

Some Christian theologians agree with them. When I was studying at Yale in the late 1960s, I had a graduate class on the philosophy of religion. Before the class got started, the conversation turned to the question of whether anyone in the room actually believed in Jesus' Resurrection. One Lutheran woman there seemed inclined to argue that it really happened, but all of the other students were on the other side. Finally, she said, "What if a couple of doctors had been there? They knew Jesus before the Crucifixion and they examined him after the Resurrection, and they said, 'This is the same guy.' Would that make any difference?"

The other students said, "Of course not."

"What about five doctors?" she asked.

They said, "No difference at all."

You see, these students were convinced, quite apart from any evidence which might be presented, that miracles cannot happen. But if miracles don't happen, Jesus is still in the tomb. Jesus is not the Messiah, not God become flesh. Jesus is just a dead blasphemer. As Paul said, "If Christ has not been raised, then our proclamation has been in vain and your faith has been in vain" (1 Cor. 15:14).

Must we choose between rigorous science or the historic Christian belief in miracles like the Incarnation and the Resurrection? I think not. I think there is a dreadful intellectual confusion here and people are making a leap of logic that is not warranted.

You see, science tells us what nature regularly does. It tells us this with amazing precision. But science can never tell us if a God created the whole natural process, including nature's laws, a God who transcends the very processes of nature, a God who could suspend those laws if He chose to do so. If the God of historic Christian faith exists, then a miracle is possible anytime that God wishes to do a miracle. So the real question is about our doctrine of God and whether we have any historical evidence that such a miracle actually happened.

I am personally trained as a historian. My Ph.D. is in history, not in theology. As a historian, I have spent a lot of time carefully examining the historical evidence for this astonishing claim that the carpenter from Nazareth was alive again on the third day, that the tomb was empty. I have come to the conclusion that, if you don't start with a philosophical prejudice against miracles, the evidence confirming this event is remarkably strong.

Some years ago, I had the opportunity to spend about two hours with the brilliant German theologian Wolfhart Pannenberg. We talked about the Resurrection and the historical methodology for investigating it. Twice in that conversation, Professor Pannenberg said that the evidence for Jesus' resurrection is so strong that no one would ever reject it except for two things: (1) it's a very unusual event, and (2) if you really think it happened, you must change the way you live.

Briefly, let us consider four historical reasons why it is intellectually responsible to believe that Jesus was alive on the third day. Then let us go one step farther and ask, "So what? What does it mean in our lives if He did rise from the dead?"

### *His Followers Were Transformed*

First of all, note the change in the disciples. Shortly after the Crucifixion, the formerly disheartened disciples announced to a Jerusalem crowd that Jesus had been raised from the dead. Within a few years, the same men proceeded to travel across the Roman Empire, braving intense persecution to tell this story. Eventually, all of the apostles, except one, were martyred. The same men had scattered at Jesus' arrest and run home in despair. What gave rise to their Resurrection faith within just a few weeks? What gave them such an amazing willingness to risk their lives to spread the gospel?

Even some skeptical scholars say there must be some explanation for this complete transformation in the apostles' behavior. One of the most fascinating comments I have found in this regard is from a famous European Jewish scholar, who believes that Jesus was alive on the third day. This is what he says:

> I am completely convinced that the Twelve from Galilee, who were all farmers, shepherds, and fishermen (there was not a single theology professor among them), were totally unimpressed by scholarly,

> sophisticated writing. If they through such a concrete historical event as the Crucifixion were totally in despair and crushed, as all the four Evangelists report to us, then no less concrete an historical event was needed to bring them up out of the valley of their deep despair and within a short time transform them into a community of salvation, rejoicing to the high heaven (Pinchas Lapide, *The Resurrection of Jesus: A Jewish Perspective*, p. 16).

The people who were closest to the event said the reason for this dramatic transformation was that they met Jesus, who changed them in astonishing ways. If you reject that explanation, you have to formulate another explanation for what happened. A famous historian at the University of Chicago said that "the origin of Christianity is almost incomprehensible unless such an event took place" (Robert Grant, *Historical Introduction to the New Testament*, p. 376).

So the first piece of evidence for the Resurrection is this amazing change in Jesus' discouraged disciples.

***His Tomb Was Empty***

Second, note the empty tomb. A very short time after the Resurrection, Peter stood up publicly in Jerusalem and said that Jesus was alive. It's significant that he made that announcement in Jerusalem. The first church arose in Jerusalem, precisely the place where anyone could have gone to visit the real burial place of Jesus. In Jerusalem hundreds of people became Christians within months of Jesus' death on the cross. Obviously, it was in the interest of the Jewish religious leaders to produce the body of Jesus—or at least give clear evidence of where it had been placed if it was no longer in the tomb. But the counterargument they offered was that the disciples had stolen Jesus' body. *That was an acknowledgment that the Jewish leaders didn't know where it was.*

There have been many attempts to explain the empty tomb of Jesus. One suggestion was that Joseph of Arimathea or the Roman soldiers or the Jewish leaders themselves removed the body before the women arrived. But if that's what happened, the Jewish leaders would have conducted guided tours to the real burial place as soon as the silly disciples started running around Jerusalem and claiming that Jesus was alive. In his discussion of Jesus' resurrection, Professor Wolfhart Pannenberg says this:

> In Jerusalem, the place of Jesus' execution and grave, it was proclaimed not long after his death that he had been raised. The situation demands that, within the circle of the first community, there was reliable testimony for the fact that the grave had been found empty. The Resurrection proclamation could not have been maintained in Jerusalem for a single day, for a single hour if the emptiness of the tomb had not been established as a fact for all concerned (Wolfhart Pannenberg, *Jesus: God and Man*, p. 100).

Since, then, the first Christians and those who disagreed with them confirm that the tomb was empty, it seems very likely that the empty tomb of Jesus is a historical fact.

### *His First Eyewitnesses Were Women*

Third, note the intriguing fact that the first people to visit the tomb and visit the risen Jesus were women. That speaks in favor of the authenticity of the Resurrection accounts. A famous professor at Cambridge, C.F.D. Moule, has said that "women were notoriously invalid witnesses according to first-century Jewish principles of evidence" ("The Significance of the Message of the Resurrection for Faith in Jesus Christ," *Studies in Biblical Theology*, 8: 9). That's the British scholar's polite way of saying that in the first century, the word of a woman was useless in court because the Jews didn't think she could get the facts straight. That's important for this reason: If the early Christians had fabricated the story about the sightings of the resurrected Jesus, they would not have said that women were the first to meet Him. That would have guaranteed that no one would believe their story. The best explanation for the priority of the women in this account is that it really happened that way, and the Gospel writers were too careful with the historical facts to change it.

### *He Had Many Other Eyewitnesses*

Fourth, note that the oldest written evidence for the Resurrection is found in 1 Corinthians (circa A.D. 50–55). Paul stated,

> I handed on to you as of first importance what I in turn had received: that Christ died for our sins in accordance with the scriptures, and that he was buried, and that he was raised on the third day in accordance with the scriptures, and that he appeared to Cephas, then to the twelve. Then he appeared to more than five hundred brothers and sisters at one time, most of whom are still alive, though some have died. Then he appeared to James, then to all the apostles. Last of all . . . he appeared also to me (15: 3–8).

Paul implied that if his readers didn't believe the Resurrection, they could check with the eyewitnesses because most of them were still around. And scholars have pointed out that Paul's words, "I handed on to you as of first importance what I in turn had received," are the words used in Jewish oral tradition to denote the very careful handing down of spiritual teaching. The Jews were very good at conveying precisely the words of a rabbi, and they used these words to signify that they were repeating that teaching verbatim. So these words about Jesus' resurrection had taken a fixed form at a very early date, probably just a few years after it occurred.

We could consider many other kinds of historical evidence for the Resurrection of Jesus, but it seems to me that there are solid historical reasons for thinking that Jesus the carpenter was no longer in His tomb on the third day.

So what? What if someone two thousand years ago rose from the dead? What does that have to do with you and me today? I think it has a lot to do with us, and I want to mention four things.

First of all, it's clear in the New Testament that the Resurrection was the decisive event that caused the early church to move from calling Jesus their Teacher to calling Him their Lord. Second, the resurrected Lord offers the inner strength for our life of costly discipleship. Third, the Resurrection is the best clue about the connection between our work now for peace and justice and the coming kingdom when Christ returns. Finally, the Resurrection is the foundation for the Christian understanding of death. Let us briefly consider each point.

### *He Is Our Lord*

The Resurrection caused the disciples to move from calling Jesus "Rabbi" and "Teacher" to calling Him "Messiah" and "Lord." In the early chapters of Acts, the Resurrection is described as the decisive event that led them to say that He was the Son of God. They now called Him *kurios*, which is the Greek word that we translate as "Lord" in English. As we noted earlier, it's the same word that Jewish scholars used when they translated the Old Testament into Greek and came to the word *Yahweh*. They translated that Hebrew word for God by using this Greek word *kurios*. This word became the most common Christian title for this carpenter from Nazareth.

Right here many modern readers take offense. Everyone is glad to acknowledge Jesus as the greatest ethical teacher of all time, the most profound peacemaker of human history. But Christians remember that Jesus said He is "the way, and the truth, and the life" (John 14:6). Jesus said that He is true God as well as true man.

If that is who Jesus is—and twenty centuries of His followers have confessed that's who He is—then we need to submit every corner of our lives to Him. We cannot pick out the parts of Jesus' teachings that feel good to us or to our friends or to our subculture, then ignore the rest. We cannot emphasize the fact that Jesus calls us to love our neighbors and liberate the poor, then forget that He also came to die for our sins. We cannot emphasize the fact that Jesus calls us to be peacemakers, then overlook that He also summons us to sexual purity. If the carpenter from Nazareth is God incarnate, then we must joyfully submit every corner of our lives to Him:

- our family budgets
- our lifestyles
- our sexual lives
- our theology
- our politics
- our economics
- our jobs

If the Peacemaker of the Sermon on the Mount is truly Lord of all things, then we cannot restrict His sovereignty to a private sphere of family, while we participate by our jobs, our research, and our votes in society's blind rush to ecological destruction or economic injustice or nuclear war. If the risen Jesus is the One who most fully showed us that God has a special concern for the poor, then Christians must work for a radical change between the scarred inner city and the pleasant suburbs, between African Americans and whites, between rich and poor nations.

If the Resurrection really happened, then it confirms that Jesus' nonviolent way of loving enemies is not some naïve utopianism, but a realistic modeling of the *shalom* of the coming kingdom. Therefore, Christians dare to engage in costly challenge to people who want to kill others. The Resurrection is the foundation for this amazing claim that the Man from Nazareth is true God as well as true man.

### *He Is Our Strength*

Second, the risen Jesus at the center of our lives gives us the strength to follow through on costly obedience and discipleship. It's not always easy to continue to work at painful marriages or to strive for peace and justice when our society is going in the other direction. It's not always easy to stick to Jesus' command to love our enemies when almost all of the TV preachers tell us it's okay to kill whenever the government says so. It's not easy to persist in living simply when so many people in our churches seem to be living by other standards. Nothing can more securely anchor our faithful commitment to the struggle for peace and justice and faithful discipleship than the regenerating presence of the risen Jesus at the center of our lives.

The apostle Paul said that Christians die to their old selves and are raised to a new life in Christ (Eph. 2:6). He said that the same supernatural power of God that raised Jesus from the dead now blows through our sinful, selfish personalities, slowly transforming us. In the power of the Resurrection we go forth to live lives of obedient discipleship, to work for peace and justice. Just as Christ died and was raised, so by faith we can die to the old life of self-centeredness and rise to a new life in Christ. Paul declared, "We have been buried with him by baptism into death, so that, just as Christ was raised from the dead by the glory of the Father, so we too might walk in newness of life" (Rom. 6:4). Or as Paul put it in Galatians, "It is no longer I who live, but it is Christ who lives in me" (2:20).

Christ in us means that we live for Christ's sake a life for others. This may mean losing a job because we will not participate in the manufacture of nuclear weapons. It may mean rejecting an attractive position in Washington in order to live with the poor in the inner city or in a developing nation. It will certainly mean being willing to risk the disapproval of parents, colleagues, even fellow church members as we side with the poor and insist on Jesus' call to be peacemakers. Because Christ lives in us, we will have the spiritual energy to do the difficult. We will be able to show the same kind of love that Christ revealed in dying for us, precisely because the God who raised Jesus now raises you and me to a new life for others.

We must not be confused at this point. I believe passionately in the importance of social justice and peacemaking, but I want to insist that we have everything confused if we suppose that the ethical teaching of Jesus is the center and essence of Christian faith. The rabbis and Confucius had taught the Golden Rule long before Jesus did. Others had advocated nonviolence. The essence of Christian faith is an I-Thou encounter. It's a personal relationship with the risen Christ, who offers us forgiveness and a new inner power to transform our self-centered personalities. He makes us part of the new community of believers who begin to live out Jesus' kingdom ethics. Of course, that kind of personal, saving faith is tied inevitably to a life of costly discipleship that includes a concern for peace and justice. But let's never reduce Christian faith to a list of Jesus' ethical teachings; that tears the power out of Christian faith. That removes the fantastic, transforming power of the risen Jesus from the center of our lives as believers.

### *He Is Our* Shalom

Third, the Resurrection offers the best clue about the relationship between our work now for peace and justice in the world and the coming *shalom* (wholeness) when Christ returns. What is the connection? Often the New Testament tells us that what happened to Jesus at His resurrection is going to happen to you and me, as well as all people who believe in Him, at the final resurrection.

This is not just an individualistic promise. Paul also noted in Romans 8 that, as the individual Christian will experience a resurrection of the body, so when Christ returns the groaning creation around us will be purged of its evil and decay to experience a total transformation. He said that creation will experience glorious freedom like that of the children of God (v. 21).

Notice the continuity and discontinuity between our work now and the coming kingdom, just as there were continuity and discontinuity between Jesus of Nazareth and the risen Jesus. Let's start by thinking about Jesus and the continuity. Jesus of Nazareth was raised bodily on the third day; it was not some chimeral resurrection in the confused minds of befuddled disciples. The man from Nazareth rose bodily from the tomb, appeared to them, talked with them, ate with them.

But there was also discontinuity in Jesus' resurrection. The risen Jesus was no longer subject to death and decay. His resurrected body did some things that we do not understand in our space-time continuum. He suddenly appeared in rooms, and so on.

I believe there is the same sort of continuity and discontinuity between human culture and history as we know it and the coming kingdom when Christ returns. Let's start with the discontinuity. We are not going to create more and more peaceful and just societies until we wake up some fine morning and realize that the kingdom has arrived. Don't believe that. There will be dreadful imperfection and sin until Christ returns.

As for the continuity, the New Testament describes the coming kingdom as "a new earth" (Rev. 21:1). According to Romans 8, the natural world around us will be restored to wholeness. The Tree of Life in the New Jerusalem is for the "healing of the nations" (Rev. 22:2), and the kings of the earth will bring their honor into the Holy City of the new kingdom. Just as Jesus of Nazareth was bodily resurrected from the dead, so too will the earth and human civilization be purged somehow of evil and taken up into the New Jerusalem at Christ's return. All will be changed, just as Jesus' body was changed. But just as it was Jesus, the man from Nazareth, who was resurrected on Easter morning, so too it will be you and me that God will transform and bring into the New Jerusalem in ways that we cannot even begin to understand now. So there is continuity between our work now and the coming kingdom, and Jesus' Resurrection provides the clue to that continuity.

### *He Is Our Promise of Eternal Life*

Finally, Jesus' resurrection is the foundation for the Christian view of death. I was stunned in my home congregation of Oxford Circle Mennonite Church when my pastor related the following: He said that a close friend works at a well-known Mennonite retirement home in Pennsylvania, and this person had discovered that many of the elderly people in that home are afraid to die. Over the ages, death has posed a terrifying threat. It is feared. But modern secular folk like to pretend otherwise.

Bertrand Russell was a well-known secular philosopher of the twentieth century, and he assured us that death ends personal existence forever. We die, we rot—that's it! No big deal! Most people buy life insurance and try to forget about it. But what ultimate meaning does personal existence possess if it persists for a mere threescore years and ten (or perhaps, by virtue of modern medicine, fourscore years) and then passes into sheer nothingness? A Marxist philosopher named Ernst Bloch said something very interesting about the modern tendency to forget about the reality of death. He said modern people can do that only because they are still living on borrowed Christian ideas. He stated that modern people are living on "a borrowed credit card." Somehow, earlier Christian ideas about life after death are still reassuring people.

Christians believe that death is not a terrifying passage into nothingness but is a transition into a glorious eternity in the presence of the risen Lord. Why do we believe that? Because one person, Jesus of Nazareth, has already experienced death in all of its fullness—even its terror—and has returned from the dead to live forevermore.

When Paul told the Corinthians that Jesus was "the first fruits of those who have died" (1 Cor. 15: 20), he meant that what happened to Jesus will, when Jesus returns, happen to all of us who believe in Him. So we await a Savior. We await the risen Lord Jesus who will change our lowly earthly bodies to become like His glorious resurrected body. That's powerfully attractive. But a little part of our minds asks, *Isn't that just wishful thinking?*

There's an interesting story about Martin Luther, the great Christian Reformer. He became very ill one time and everyone thought he was going to die, but he got better unexpectedly. His friends asked how he felt when he came face-to-face with death. Luther's first response as a good theologian was that he believed that death did not mark the end of his existence. He said, "I believe that Jesus will restore me to life."

Then Luther added with a slow smile, "Natural reason says that is a preposterous lie."

We all understand that a part of our minds is inclined to wonder. Without strong evidence to support the belief in life after death, we might not believe it. Christians have faith in the Resurrection because it has already happened. We believe that death is not a terrifying threat because Jesus' tomb is empty. The One with whom the disciples had lived has appeared to them and assured them that He is alive forevermore. He or she who trusts in the Lord can declare with Paul,

> "Death has been swallowed up in victory."
> "Where, O death, is your victory?
> Where, O death, is your sting?" . . .
> Thanks be to God, who gives us the victory through our Lord Jesus Christ.
> (1 Cor. 15:55–57)

My dad told me the following story, which provides a marvelous illustration of our confidence in the risen Christ. Mom had lived a healthy life and had not experienced a lot of pain, but in her last week she did have a good deal of pain and she was obviously declining. On a Friday evening, Dad was sitting beside the couch where Mom was resting, and he was holding her hand. Rather quietly, Mom said, "I think I'll just go and be with Jesus."

Dad fought back the tears and said, "That's right. You do that. And I'm going to pray right now that you can go real soon." Twenty-four hours later, she was dead.

With this view of death—with this assurance of the Resurrection—we can look death in the face without fear. With this view of death we can also live courageously today. You see, "life at any cost" is not the Christian motto. Death in the King's cause is not disastrous. Paul said that if we live, we live to the Lord, and if we die, we die to the Lord: "For to this end Christ died and lived again, so that he might be Lord of both the dead and the living" (Rom. 14:9).

Because Christ is Lord of the living and the dead, we dare to face racists and militarists in His name. We dare to do it for the sake of our sisters and brothers who need us. We dare to go as missionaries into dangerous situations to spread the gospel. We dare to leave comfortable classrooms and go into struggling nations as volunteers to help those people experience justice and wholeness. If we live, we live to the Lord. And if we die, we die to the Lord. He is the King, the Lord even of death.

Jesus of Nazareth rose from the dead. That is not just a fascinating item of ancient history. Jesus' resurrection is the foundation of our belief that the carpenter of Nazareth is the Lord of the whole universe. A living relationship with this risen Lord Jesus provides us the strength for our daily walk of obedience in discipleship. Jesus' resurrection provides us an important clue about the relationship between our work now for a better world and the perfection that will surely come when Christ returns. The risen Jesus is powerful evidence that even that last terror, death itself, will be but for a moment. In the words of the wonderful song, every Christian can say,

> Because He lives, I can face tomorrow.
> Because He lives, all fear is gone.
> Because I know He holds the future,
> And life is worth the living
> Just because He lives.*

---

*William J. Gaither and Gloria Gaither, "Because He Lives," *Hymns for Praise and Worship* (Nappanee, IN: Evangel Press, 1984), no. 494.